CH00664796

Advance P₁

Extreme

"It will behoove readers who care about justice to follow the guidance of Judge Steve Dankof as he sweeps back and forth across history to make the administration of our laws—in all their Byzantine complexities—understandable. This is a gifted chronicler who cares about the times in which we must endure."

—**Wil Haygood**, author of **SHOWDOWN**:
Thurgood Marshall and the Supreme Court
Nomination that Changed America

"The great Frederick Douglass said, in another trying time for our democracy and the rule of law: 'It is not light that is needed, but the fire; not the gentle shower, but the thunder. We need the storm, the whirlwind, the earthquake—the conscience of the nation must be roused.' Judge Steve Dankof, in this terrific little book, is the thunder, not the gentle shower."

—**Gene Nichol**, Tinsley Distinguished Professor of Law,
University of North Carolina, author of **THE FACES OF
POVERTY IN NORTH CAROLINA** and
INDECENT ASSEMBLY

"Judge Steven K. Dankof pulls no punches in this extraordinarily honest and critical examination of judicial responsibility in wrongful convictions. *Extreme Cruelty* should be required reading for everyone working in the courts and anyone interested in a meaningful dialogue about criminal justice reform. I could not put this book down."

—**Gilbert King**, Pulitzer Prize winner for
DEVIL IN THE GROVE: Thurgood Marshall,
the Groveland Boys, and the Dawn of a New America

Extreme Cruelty

The Complicity of Judges in the Shame of Wrongful Convictions

Judge Steven Dankof

proving press

Book Design & Production:
Columbus Publishing Lab
www.ColumbusPublishingLab.com

Cover design by Nancy Dankof

Hardback ISBN: 978-1-63337-800-1
Paperback ISBN: 978-1-63337-798-1
Ebook ISBN: 978-1-63337-799-8

Printed in the United States of America
1 3 5 7 9 10 8 6 4 2

CONTENTS

For Nancy and our family.

Foreword

By Mark Godsey[1]

I FIRST MET JUDGE STEVEN DANKOF in 2013 through my representation of Dean Gillispie, an innocent man who served 20 years in prison for rapes he didn't commit. Dankof had inherited Dean's case when he took over the docket of his predecessor, the late Judge AJ Wagner. As Director of the Ohio Innocence Project (OIP), I had worked on Dean's case for a decade by the time I met Dankof. In 2011, Dean had been freed after serving 20 years in prison when a federal court threw out his conviction because the police hid, destroyed or lost evidence in their file that eliminated him as a suspect. In 2012, an Ohio appellate court threw out his conviction a second time in response to strong evidence we had presented showing that someone else likely committed the offense. Dean is the only person I've ever heard of who had his conviction thrown out on two completely independent grounds.

---

1. Daniel P. and Judith L. Carmichael Professor of Law, University of Cincinnati College of Law, and Director, Rosenthal Institute for Justice/Ohio Innocence Project.

The case fell into Judge Dankof's lap in early 2013 only because the prosecutors wanted to retry Dean, with no reliable evidence. The problem for the prosecutors was that the federal judge who had tossed out Dean's convictions and freed him had already said they could not retry him. It would violate the constitution to do so, said the federal judge. But the prosecutors didn't care. In a move reminiscent of Alabama Supreme Court justice Roy Moore when he ordered probate judges in Alabama to refuse to issue marriage licenses to same-sex couples following Obergefell v. Hodges--claiming that he had the power to defy the U.S. Supreme Court - Dean's prosecutors in essence gave the middle finger to the federal bench and the Supremacy Clause of the U.S. Constitution and said, "We don't care. We'll do what we want. We'll tell our state court judges to ignore the orders of the federal courts."

And if AJ Wagner had still been the judge on Dean's case, the prosecutors likely would have gotten away with it. Dean's case had been before Wagner for years prior to his retirement, and he had gone out of his way to ignore clear constitutional violations and evidence of Dean's innocence in order to give the appearance that our criminal justice system doesn't make terrible mistakes, and to keep Dean in prison. Sadly, far too many elected state court judges like Wagner, following their "tough on crime" election vows, are loath to defy the prosecution in high stakes, high-profile cases. Although we ultimately overturned Wagner's decisions twice, his biases and refusal to follow the law kept Dean in prison an additional four years.

But in 2013, I soon learned that Dankof was of a different cloth. Unlike his predecessor, he took the matter very seriously. He ordered extensive briefing from the parties. He held hearings and oral arguments. And he eventually issued a decision upholding the rule of law, barring the prosecutor's attempts to put Dean through an unconstitutional "vengeance retrial," and dismissing the indictment against Dean. But that was just the first of many courageous things Judge Dankof did thereafter. Following that decision, he conducted an in-camera inspection of the original grand jury testimony in the case, which helped further lay bare the police misconduct in the case.

Since that time, Judge Dankof has become a national leader on the bench, devising ways that judges can combat the scourge of wrongful convictions. Always on the cutting edge, he has drafted jury instruction that help jurors understand problems with human memory, eyewitness identification, implicit bias, and many other important problems that our judicial system has ignored for decades. He has time and time again stuck his neck out for, as he calls it, "actual, authentic, real due process." Judge Dankof is, in my opinion, a judicial hero.

In this book, you will see Dankof's conviction, courage, and what makes him unique. This is an important read for anyone who cares about justice. I wish more judges would think and act like Judge Dankof, and I truly hope this book will encourage them to do so.

Prologue

"In the country of my birth, which is England, a judge is someone who comes at you from antiquity...A wretch who died in the time of Dickens would easily recognize the legal procedure of the ancient regime in the present day."

CHRISTOPHER HITCHENS

BY MAY 2017, I'd already been a trial judge on the Montgomery County Ohio Common Pleas Court's General Division for roughly six years. As a result, I was entirely familiar with the phenomenon of wrongful convictions, both in the Montgomery County Common Pleas Court specifically, and Ohio and American Courts generally.

Necessarily, then, I had become aware of the tireless efforts of the Ohio Innocence Project to free Ohioans languishing in prison, wrongly convicted of crimes of which they were innocent.

As I stood in the checkout line at my local grocery that day in May, I couldn't miss the magazine rack prominently displaying a Special TIME Edition: ***INNOCENT – The Fight Against Wrongful Convictions – 25 Years of the Innocence Project***. Quickly thumbing through the magazine, I saw articles about two men I had come to know: Rickey Jackson and Mark Godsey. Naturally, I bought a copy, which still adorns my chambers.

At age 18, Rickey Jackson was convicted of murdering Harold Franks[1], landing on Ohio's Death Row based entirely on the "synthesized"[2] eyewitness testimony of 12-year-old middle schooler Edward Vernon, coerced by the Cleveland Police Department to lie. Before his November 2014 exoneration, Rickey spent 39 years in prison, too many on Death Row, until Edward Vernon admitted he'd not even witnessed the murder. When young Edward tried to recant his statement, Cleveland police told him it was "too late" and that if he recanted, Edward's parents would be arrested for perjury. Those same Cleveland police that, at the time, knew full well that two other men, Paul Gardenshire and Ishmael Hixon, were suspected of involvement in the Franks murder.

The Cleveland police never moved forward to investigate cases against Gardenshire and Hixon despite Hixon's past record, including a shooting and robbery, and the fact

---

1. The following true story of Rickey Jackson's wrongful conviction and imprisonment is informed entirely by Courtney Mifusd's wonderful article, *A Lifetime Lost, Then Freedom* in *TIME: INNOCENT – The Fight Against Wrongful Convictions* (May, 2017) and Rickey's own account: *My Life on Death Row* in the same edition.

2. Which is to say perjury, suborned by the Cleveland Police.

that the license plate of the getaway car matched Hixon's. A year after Franks' murder, Hixon pleaded guilty to more than a dozen counts of aggravated robbery. So it goes… Whence, then, so many judges' childlike embrace of all law enforcement as "blue knights"?

Rickey came within two months of his execution date, and was only spared the gallows by virtue of the court's mistake in filling out his death penalty paperwork. Serendipity, as opposed to divine intervention, had spared Rickey's life. Bridgeman and Ajamu, Rickey's co-defendants, escaped their death sentences only because the U.S. Supreme Court struck down Ohio's death-penalty statute as unconstitutional. One of the men came within a *week* of his execution date.

Rickey's lawyer was University of Cincinnati Law Professor Mark Godsey, Director of Ohio's Innocence Project.

These days, I'm in my 14th year on the Bench, and while I don't make the kind of money I once did as a Plaintiff's personal injury lawyer,[3] I have the best job for which I could have ever hoped.

Notwithstanding, on far too many days, I'm sorely tempted to smash myself in the face with my gavel.

Why, you may ask?

---

3. To the occasionally expressed chagrin of Mrs. Dankof…

Because so much of what is done by and in the Criminal Justice System, more properly dubbed the "Criminal *Injustice* System" or the "Punishment Bureaucracy" by Alec Karakatsanis in his excellent book, **Usual Cruelty**[4], has absolutely no foundation or underpinning in empirical evidence. Doing things for which there is no empirical underpinning is especially reprehensible in a time when the gathering of data and its analysis is at our finger tips, owing to the miracles of IT.

Sadly, judges and their courts do most things because, well, "that's the way we've always done things around here", and because appellate courts give their *imprimatur* to Hitchens' "Ancient Regime", despite knowing full well that "those ways", in reality, do not, cannot, and **were never intended** to fulfill a judge's sacred responsibilities embedded in the Constitution and the Bill of Rights. No, "those ways" were and are intended to maintain the *status quo* which is more concerned with the **appearance** of constitutional rigor rather than actually adhering to the lofty, stated goals of our nation's seminal documents.

In criminal law, **Blackstone's Ratio** is the notion that:

> "It is better that ten guilty persons escape than that one innocent suffer."[5]

---

4. The New Press, 2019.

5. Similar sentiments were expressed by Voltaire in 1749 and later Franklin in his 1785 letter to Benjamin Vaughan.

Sentient trial judges know that reality and the truth bear no resemblance to **Blackstone's Ratio.** The complicity and conspiracy of the Executive, Judicial, and Legislative branches of our state and federal governments buttress, day after day, our willingness to consign the innocent and wrongfully convicted to the horrors of mass incarceration in an unconstitutional crusade to **ensure** not a single guilty person escapes our greedy clutches. Let's call this the **Reality Ratio,** which has the actual effect of allowing the truly guilty to go free and remain at large.

Can we be brutally honest: we know that **we have executed innocent people**, don't we?

The acceptance of this reality, that innocent living, breathing fellow *sapiens* have died at our hands, should haunt us unto the grave.

The doing of things as they've always been done without empirical evidence to support those things is the product of *hubris*, desperation, or sloth. Perhaps all three. But, in any event, and much like American Foreign Policy, doing things as they've always been done is doomed to failure.

Speaking of empirical data, here's a bit to wrap your heads around. The Land of the Free and the Home of the Brave is the greatest mass incarcerator in the history of the world, both in terms of total persons incarcerated and persons incarcerated per 100,000 of population. Massachusetts, the state with the *lowest* U.S. incarceration rate, would rank 17th *highest* in the world per 100,000 of population, ahead of such bastions of hope as Saudi Arabia, China, Iran, Columbia, and Russia.[6]

As we begin our journey together through these pages, I merely note the obvious: contributing to the abomination of mass U.S. incarceration are wrongful convictions that necessarily result in wrongful imprisonment.

In Fall 2019, I spoke at an Ohio Innocence Project event in Cincinnati, along with an appellate judge and a former prosecuting attorney, to address why wrongful convictions keep happening and with such unrelenting frequency.

At the outset of the evening, I'd managed to get my fellow participants to agree that I would go last – always better to play off the other speakers and have the last word, don't you think?

So, in the remaining time allotted to me, I spoke to the nice people who'd come to support the work of the Innocence Project and *honestly* answered their queries because, as I explained, I considered them friends in the quest for justice – and friends should speak *honestly* with one another.

---

6. Prison Policy Initiative, September, 2021.

In that vein and spirit, I told them to take a good, hard look at me because I and my fellow trial judges were the problem: we were the cause of the unrelenting wrongful convictions and imprisonment.

Let me repeat myself, at the considerable risk of alienating many of my fellow trial judges, and posit the unassailable:

Trial Judges are the primary cause of wrongful convictions and resulting wrongful imprisonment.

This book is not another catechism, full of musty "truisms" on how to be fair and impartial. Rather, this little book is a polemic, a call to arms, if you will, directed primarily at fellow trial judges. And if I'm lucky, a new generation of law students embarking upon their legal journey who may glean from these pages ways to hold trial judges to their oaths and, in all events, unflinchingly preserve for the record the trial judge's errors and sins, hoping *somehow* for meaningful appellate review, by demonstrating that those errors and sins weren't merely harmless or immaterial, and that evidence of guilt was anything but overwhelming...

My polemic makes no pretense at flyspecking and parsing the science and data relating to each factor that I believe contributes to wrongful convictions and imprisonment. Take, for example, the real phenomenon of **False Confession,** which contributes mightily to wrongful convictions and imprisonment. The fact that many judges flatly disbelieve that False Confession is a "real thing" is disturbing enough. That so many of us can't be bothered to consult seminal works on the subject to inform ourselves is shameful.

My polemic is not a "measured" academic treatise. Its purpose is to provoke strong reaction from judges of all stripes, but particularly my fellows on the trial bench, even if that initial reaction is pushback, rejection and anger.

Ever the dreamer, I believe that from strong reaction, new ways of thought and thus essential pathways to meaningful change may spring that, in the end, empower trial judges to do all that they can to stem the flow of wrongful convictions and imprisonment.

To breathing life into our judicial oaths.

Because, in the end, the only effective bulwark against wrongful convictions and imprisonment are sentient trial judges, providing *actual, authentic,* and *real* Due Process and Fundamental Fairness to the Accused.

It sure won't be the Executive or Legislative Branches, much less the appellate courts.

Here goes.

1.

The Scourge and Shame of Wrongful Convictions

"And before Dantes could open his mouth…the jailer disappeared, taking with him the lamp and closing the door, leaving stamped upon the prisoner's mind the dim reflection of the dripping walls of his dungeon."

The Count of Monte Cristo, BY ALEXANDRE DUMAS

ASIDE FROM PREDATION, *isolation* – the very essence of wrongful conviction and imprisonment – is humankind's greatest fear. Is it any wonder, then, that Dumas' novel, ***The Count of Monte Cristo***,[1] remains the most oft-revisited, quintessential story of injustice, revenge, and redemption?

But truth is nearly always more compelling than fiction.

The true story of the wrongful conviction of French artillery officer Alfred Dreyfus and his life sentence to the Devil's Island penal colony in French Guiana in 1895, fueled as it was by overt antisemitism, sparked political

---

1. First published in 1844 and the subject of dozens of film versions.

and social upheaval in the French Third Republic before Dreyfus' ultimate exoneration in 1906. The Dreyfus Affair remains fresh in the memory to this day.[2]

The National Registry of Exonerations and the Innocence Project report, as of April 25, 2023, over 575[3] **_DNA exonerations_** in the United States, meaning that DNA evidence has established, **_beyond any doubt_**, that a prisoner was wrongfully convicted and imprisoned. Those 575 DNA exonerations **_include 35 people exonerated from Death Row_**.

Importantly, DNA exonerations are the mere tip of the wrongful conviction iceberg, as Saul Kassin, Ph.D. underscores in his brilliant book **_Duped_**[4] because most crimes do not present testable traces of DNA, and in those crimes that do, DNA samples are often contaminated, destroyed, or otherwise unavailable.

Innocence Project statistics regarding the first 375 definitive DNA wrongful conviction exonerations are revealing:

---

2. *Why the Dreyfus Affair Matters*, by Louis Begley, Yale Press (2009).

3. Including 196 Innocence Project clients. DNA and Wrongful Conviction: Five Facts You Should Know; The Innocence Project, April 25, 2023, by Daniele Selby.

4. *Duped* - Why Innocent People Confess - and Why We Believe Their Confessions, by Saul Kassin, Ph.D., Prometheus (2022)

1. The ***average years of wrongful imprisonment – 14***;
2. Total years of wrongful imprisonment – 5,284;
3. 21 of the 375 ***served time on death row***;
4. 69% involved ***eyewitness misidentification***, of which 42% involved ***cross-racial misidentification***;
5. 43% involved "misapplication of forensic science" or ***"junk science,"*** including discredited "disciplines" such as bite marks, footprints, hair comparisons, various arson theories, comparative bullet lead analysis, etc.;
6. 29% involved ***false confession***, virtually half of which were by confessors 21 years of age or younger at the time of their arrest;
7. 20% involved ***jailhouse informants-snitches***;
8. Ultimately 165 actual assailants were identified;
9. Demographics of the wrongfully convicted: 60% African American; 31% Caucasian; 8% Latinx.

As of April 11, 2024, the Home Page for The National Registry of Exonerations[5] states there have been ***3,499 exonerations*** since 1989, reflecting ***more than***

---

5. A joint project of the Newkirk Center for Science & Society at UC Irvine, the University of Michigan School of Law and the Michigan State University College of Law.

31,900 years of wrongful imprisonment. The National Registry's statistics regarding these wrongful convictions are similarly revealing:

1. 64% involved perjury or false accusation;
2. 60%[6] involved ***official misconduct*** – like threatening to prosecute a young boy's parents if he won't stick to a "synthesized" story ginned up by law enforcement;
3. 27% involved mistaken witness ID;
4. 25% involved false or misleading forensic evidence;
5. 13% involved false confession;
6. 53% of those wrongfully convicted were African American.

As of March 22, 2023, Ohio alone sported 104 exonerations since 1989, with more than 1,040 years lost to wrongful imprisonment.[7] Ohio's Cuyahoga County "leads" the way with 26 exonerations in the first 2400 national Exonerations. In 2023 alone, at least 5 more Ohioans were exonerated, including Wayne Braddy,

---

6. Indeed, if one includes judicial misconduct, intentional or unwitting, 100% of wrongful convictions involve official misconduct.

7. UC News, Cedric Ricks, March 22, 2023.

Karl Willis, Richard Horton, Marcus Sapp, and Marty Levingston, after collectively serving 90 years in prison.[8]

My trial court, the Montgomery County Common Pleas Court, has its own share of wrongful convictions and imprisonment.

In January 1985, Jennifer Wilcox and Robert Aldridge were sentenced to life in prison following their convictions by a Montgomery County jury on multiple counts of rape and gross sexual imposition of children under 13 years of age. The wrongful convictions unraveled following admission by the State's key witnesses, young brothers, that they had falsely testified against Wilcox and Aldridge owing to relentless coercion from the lead detective and other police.

Moreover, the State had failed to disclose ***Brady***[9] material: medical evidence indicating that none of the alleged victims showed the slightest sign of sexual abuse. After each served ***more than 11 years in prison***, Wilcox and Aldridge were released. Ultimately, the State dismissed the charges, and Aldridge's and Wilcox's claims for

---

8. Ohio Innocence Project statistics quoted in "The Voice of Black Cincinnati", September 22, 2023.

9. *Brady v. Maryland,* 373 U.S. 83 (1963) holding that the State has a constitutional duty to disclose evidence that is exculpatory to a criminal defendant or which can be used by the defendant for impeachment purposes.

state compensation were settled for $800,000 and $1.1 Million, respectively.[10]

In December 1988, a Montgomery County jury convicted Tyrone Zinkiewicz of taking nude photographs of a juvenile. The judge sentenced Mr. Zinkiewicz to 5 to 15 years in prison after denying defense counsel's motions seeking to use exculpatory evidence that the testifying youth was considerably less than truthful.

Mr. Zinkiewicz's conviction was upheld in the 2nd District Court of Appeals, notwithstanding a strongly worded dissent harshly criticizing law enforcement for false representations and omissions in a search warrant application and failing to disclose the youth was under investigation for numerous serious crimes at the time he testified against Mr. Zinkiewicz. U.S. Magistrate Judge Michael Merz recommended granting a writ of *habeas corpus,* and Federal Judge Walter Rice did just that, releasing Mr. Zinkiewicz on January 29, 1992, after he'd served **more than 3 years in prison**. The prosecution dismissed the charges in May 1992.[11]

On May 1, 2009, a Montgomery County Common Pleas judge convicted Scott Chessman of violating Ohio's sex offender registration law. Ultimately, Mr. Chessman's

---

10. The National Registry of Exonerations.

11. Id.

conviction was reversed, and he was released from prison in July 2010, after serving *over a year in prison*. In 2014, the State of Ohio agreed to pay Mr. Chessman $82,000 in compensation as the result of his wrongful conviction and imprisonment.

On February 12, 1991, a Montgomery County jury convicted Dean Gillispie of raping three women in two separate events. Before sentencing, the trial judge granted Mr. Gillispie a new trial owing to newly discovered evidence.

At his second trial, Mr. Gillispie was again convicted, this time after the trial judge gave the jury, reportedly deadlocked 8-4 *for acquittal*, a "dynamite" charge[12]. The trial judge sentenced Mr. Gillispie to prison for 22 to 56 years. The 2nd District affirmed the conviction in 1993.

For more than a decade, Mr. Gillispie suffered through a series of unsuccessful petitions for new trial and other state appellate relief before filing a *federal* petition for a writ of *habeas corpus* based upon *Brady* violations *after* the 2nd District had denied relief on that very basis.

In April 2012, Judge Merz granted Mr. Gillispie's *habeas* petition and ordered a new trial based upon the

---

12. An instruction authorized by the Ohio Supreme Court in *State v. Howard*, 42 Ohio St. 3d 18 (1989), at best cajoling, and at worst coercing jurors to resume deliberations and bring back a verdict! We shall return to *Howard* in Chapter Eight.

State's failure to provide **Brady** material. With egg dripping from its collective faces, the 2nd District hastily, and only then, granted Mr. Gillispie a new trial, not for **Brady** violations, but on the basis of "alternate suspect".[13]

By this time, I had become Mr. Gillispie's state court trial judge, owing to my appointment by Gov. Strickland. In November 2016, after the State failed to produce the **Brady** material as ordered by Judge Merz, I granted Mr. Gillispie's motion to dismiss the indictment, a decision ultimately upheld in the Ohio Supreme Court.

Thereafter, Mr. Gillispie filed a civil suit in federal court seeking compensation wherein a jury, in November 2022, awarded him **$45 Million** against, among others, the Miami Township Case Detective and the Miami Township Police Department, apparently in no small part owing to my order granting his request for the grand jury testimony of the case detective that contributed mightily to his original indictment.

Mr. Gillispie also filed suit in the Montgomery County Common Pleas Court in March 2019, seeking a declaration that he was a "wrongfully imprisoned individual" under the Ohio Revised Code. The trial judge

---

13. This recounting of the Dean Gillispie "journey" is largely informed by the National Registry of Exonerations as well as Judge Merz' December 15, 2011 Decision and Order Granting Conditional Writ of *Habeas Corpus*.

assigned this latter case justified her denial of Mr. Gillispie's motion to transfer the case to me, notwithstanding my far greater familiarity with the case, on the basis of "random assignment" of cases. She then proceeded to "run out the clock" by sitting on the case, doing essentially nothing, until the literal eve of her retirement, at which time, and apparently no longer in the thrall of "random assignment", she attempted unsuccessfully to transfer the case[14] away from her successor, Judge Susan Solle.

Ultimately, in December 2021, Judge Solle declared Mr. Gillispie a wrongfully imprisoned individual pursuant to the Ohio Revised Code, thereby permitting him to proceed with his civil action against the State of Ohio[15] for compensation.

Quite simply, wrongful convictions and imprisonment are hardly novel occurrences nationally, in Ohio generally, or in Montgomery County specifically. And the flow of wrongful convictions and imprisonment continues unabated.

Maybe we should convene a Task force!

Better yet, let's embrace the simple notion that the ***actual, authentic, real*** change necessary to staunch the flow of wrongful convictions and imprisonment isn't

---

14. For reasons I can only imagine...

15. Which claim has since been settled.

coming from another Task Force, the appellate courts, or the Executive or Legislative Branches of government.

American judges all take oaths before assuming office. The Oxford English Dictionary defines "Oath" as:

> "*a solemn promise* about one's future actions or behavior; a sworn declaration, such as the promise to tell the truth…"[16]

In short, American judges *give their word* that, upon taking office, they will do certain things.

The oath of office for Ohio judges is instructive:

> "I do solemnly swear that I will support the Constitution of the United States and the Constitution of Ohio, will *administer justice* without respect to persons, and will faithfully and impartially discharge and perform all the duties incumbent upon me according to the best of my ability."[17]

The Oxford English Dictionary defines "Justice" as:

> "… the administration of law in a way that is fair and morally right."

Hanging in my courtroom, directly across from the

---

16. Emphasis mine.

17. Ohio Revised Code Section 3.23, emphasis mine.

jury box and thus in full view of the jury throughout their service, is a large poster proclaiming a famous John Lewis quotation:

> *"If you see something that is not right, not fair, not just, you have a moral obligation to do something about it."*

Dear Reader, if you are a judge and feel that this John Lewis quotation has no business in a courtroom, perhaps you have absolutely no business being a judge.

Any Ohio school child of average intelligence understands the oath, ***the solemn promise***, undertaken by Ohio's judges. And those same school children understand the meaning of "Justice".

Yet many Ohio[18] judges apparently consider their solemn promise to support the Constitutions and administer justice merely aspirational – given that they routinely disregard their oaths in a myriad of ways, thereby serving as the wellspring for the unrelenting flow of wrongful convictions and imprisonment.

Why do I say such a provocative thing?

Quite simply because it is true – as we shall see…

_____

18. I levy these same charges against judges throughout America. I focus primarily on Ohio judges and Ohio jurisprudence for the ease of illustration and brevity's blessings.

2

Pretending to Care—
The Empty Hope of Appellate Review

"You're the Supreme Court, the Supreme Court, the Supreme
Court; remember it's all of us or none; From the mountains,
to the alleys, to the maximum-security facilities, you
were sworn to be the lighthouse for the least of these,
until there are no least of these…"

THE SUPREME COURT
Little Prayers Trilogy– song by Chip Taylor[1]

"…No voices to guide us, no angels beside us; No shaman, no
mystical light; No omens, no compass, no seer, no prophet;
No Calvary coming in sight; But we're all right…"

WE'RE ALL RIGHT–*song by Mary Chapin Carpenter*

FROM TIME TO TIME, fellow trial judges have expressed
to me, in one fashion or another, that they intend to han-
dle a particularly vexing evidentiary or procedural problem
by "just letting the evidence in and leaving it up to the jury.
And if they get it wrong, the court of appeals will fix it."

There's a concept: the trial judge, at the very least

---

1. Jon Voight's little brother.

sporting undergraduate and law school diplomas and charged with the solemn promise of supporting the Constitutions and administering the law in a way that is fair and morally right, is going to go all Pontius Pilate and entrust some appellate court to right any wrongs the judge himself or a jury of well-meaning lay people might make.

Seriously?

Very early in my so-called career[2] as a trial lawyer for living, breathing human beings, I attended almost every year *The Advocacy Institute,* a wonderful 3-day trial seminar in Ann Arbor at the University of Michigan Law School, where I first encountered Gerry Spence, the great Wyoming trial lawyer. Gerry's intellect and passion, not to mention his palpable advocacy skills, were immediately inspiring to the young lawyer who writes for you now as an old man. Subsequently, I've read any number of Gerry's books[3] which advanced my representation of those living, breathing human beings in Ohio courtrooms.

In October 1998, I personally met Gerry at the University of Akron School of Law's Annual Dean's Club Dinner, courtesy of an invitation from my dear friend, Dana K. Cole, now a tenured law professor at Akron.

---

2. From 1976 until January, 2011, some 35 years.

3. Such as *How to Argue and Win Every Time*, by Gerry Spence, St. Martin's Press, 1995.

At some point during the evening, an interlocutor in the audience asked Gerry what he thought of the American *legal education* system. As I'd seen Gerry do in Ann Arbor years before, he asked first if the audience "wanted an answer". Upon receiving a resounding "YES!", Gerry asked if the audience "*really* wanted an answer". After another enthusiastic "YES!", he set the hook: "Do I have your *permission* to give you an answer?" Assured yet again, Gerry intoned that American law schools placed entirely too much emphasis on LSAT[4] test results in their selection of new students and rhetorically asked:

> "What, exactly, does the LSAT measure? It certainly doesn't measure courage, earnestness, honor, integrity and perseverance. No, the LSAT measures only one thing: who's good at clever little word games. And that's a sorry way to pick our next generation of warriors for the people."

Proof of Gerry's righteous conclusion is the cautionary tale of one John Yoo.

Mr. Yoo received his BA from Harvard and his JD from Yale. Do you suppose that Mr. Yoo did just fine on the LSAT and that, if not the very best at clever little word games, it wouldn't take too long to call the roll?

---

4. Law School Admission Test (LSAT). Recently, many of America's most elite law schools are openly abandoning the LSAT.

And for what is Mr. Yoo most renowned? That's right, his infamous "Torture Memos" in which he compliantly did the bidding of his political masters – Bush, Cheney and Rumsfeld – opining to their collective glee that waterboarding, *somehow*, wasn't torture. And for his fealty to legal sophistry and his political masters, Mr. Yoo is now the Emanuel S. Heller Professor of Law at the University of California Berkeley's august law school – Boalt Hall – where, presumably, he counsels and instructs a new generation of LSAT whiz kids as they climb the ladder of service to a grateful nation…

As a nomadic military brat and moving with my family every 3 to 4 years, whether we needed it or not, I developed "strategies" to cope with repeatedly bidding *adieu* to friends and foes alike and starting anew in, say, Montgomery, Alabama, when **The Colonel**, my late father Col. Karl E. Dankof, USAF, who lies buried at Arlington, commenced his studies in 1963 at the War College at Maxwell AFB. By any account, 1963 was a seismic year in American history. In April, Dr. King languished, presumably without bail or bond, in that Birmingham jail, penning his magisterial letter. In November, President Kennedy was murdered in Dallas. Things had, as they say, taken a turn… Some 35 years later, my Father confided that he could have gone to the War College in Newport, Rhode Island, but inexplicably chose Montgomery instead. There's a joke in there somewhere about military intelligence.

Returning to coping strategies, one I've employed throughout my life has been to assess a room full of new faces, such as fellow students in a new school. Until my first day in 1973 at The University of Texas at Austin School of Law – Townes Hall – I would survey the classroom or lecture hall at my new school and tell myself, again, that I was the smartest son of a bitch in the room. And while that wasn't necessarily true, it remains a great coping strategy to this day.

But during the first gathering of my TQ,[5] we did as we were told and dutifully stood and stated our name and undergraduate *alma mater*. After listening to my new classmates proudly announce their undergraduate journeys at places like Annapolis, Columbia, Harvard, MIT, West Point and Yale, I muttered that I was a recent graduate of The Ohio University in Athens, the oldest public university west of the Allegheny Mountains, as opposed to the cow college in Columbus with the professional football team.

As it turned out, all was well because, although I hadn't graduated from one of America's elite colleges or universities, I was entirely capable of detecting academic and intellectual horse hockey.

---

5. At UT Law, we were assigned to Teaching Quizmaster (TQ) sections and a law school senior to mentor us throughout that fateful first year.

In Constitutional Law taught by Lucas A. ("Scott") Powe, Jr. – a Yalie and former clerk for U.S. Supreme Court Associate Justice William O. Douglas, no slouch himself at clever word games[6] – it took me precious little time to realize that, in case after "seminal" case, the United States Supreme Court Justices just made it up! They had an ideological bent and thus a predetermined result they were going to reach, come hell or high water, and, despite legal precedent and lofty notions of *stare decisis*, spun a web of academic sophistry, if not downright deceit, to get where they and their political masters wanted to go.

One of my classmates at UT was Gene Ray Nichol who stood up that first day, adorned in overalls, and announced he'd just graduated from Oklahoma State – "Okie Lite". I sure wasn't worried about being outwitted by Gene.

Turns out, I should have been.

Gene Nichol is the Boyd Tinsley Distinguished Professor of Law at UNC Chapel Hill, and former President of The College of William & Mary. Gene is a personal hero to many of us in UT Law School's 1976 Graduating class. If you want to know why, just "Google" Gene and you'll find his soaring letter of Resignation from his William & Mary Presidency and grasp the level of his

---

6. Recall **"penumbras",** if you will.

personal courage in the face of vicious personal attacks because he'd presumed to "do what was right", including giving the 1st Amendment's Establishment Clause its "plain meaning" as it related to displaying a Christian Cross in a meeting hall at a *public* university.

In his book ***The Faces of Poverty in North Carolina***,[7] Gene distilled *honest* Constitutional interpretation and scholarship to its essence:

> "American constitutional law works at the intersection of aspiration, of officially declared commitment, and of a frequently value-transgressing reality. It explores – or at least it should – both what we profess and what we allow to occur, what we say and what, in reality, we do. It seeks a corrective when our practices veer too wildly from our declared promises. It triggers a remedy when undergirding presupposition hides cruel violation, when promises of full membership go consistently and pervasively unsecured. The chasm that sometimes exists between our collective social boasts and our acceptance of marginalization and exclusion can frequently be best illuminated through the jarring stories of our sisters and brothers."

---

7. The University of North Carolina Press, 2018.

Now an Ohio Common Pleas General Division trial judge, my epiphany reached so very long ago in Austin is reinforced every time my intelligence is insulted by the likes of Alito, Thomas, Barrett, etc.[8] Or every time I read another missive from the Ohio Supreme Court or one of its appellate courts, lovingly embracing *res judicata* and the finality of judgments at the expense of delivering **actual, authentic, real** Due Process to the Accused. How else to explain the penchant of appellate courts to offer up their witches' brew of "abuse of discretion review", "*de novo* review", "plain error", "structural error", "prejudicial error", "procedural error", "fundamental error", "invited error", "harmless error", "reversible error", "cumulative error", "constitutional trial error" and "overwhelming evidence of guilt"[9], etc., to justify turning a blind eye to wrongful convictions and the trial judge's obvious mistakes and errors spawning them?

Make no mistake, it is fealty to the finality of judgments, even at the cost of human life and liberty, that is the overarching aim and mission of the appellate courts.

Do I exaggerate? You tell me, Brothers and Sisters of the Bench.

---

8. Yes, I'm a liberal. But fear not. I freely admit the "High" Court's left-leaning justices are every bit as adroit at conjuring up preordained results.

9. The only thing missing from this list is "Intergalactic error"…

In 2005, John Montenegro Cruz was convicted of murdering a Tucson police officer and sentenced to death despite the U.S. Supreme Court's decision, eleven years earlier in **Simmons v. South Carolina** that, when prosecutors argue for the death penalty based upon future "dangerousness", defendants have the right to let the jury know that an alternative to the death penalty could be life without any possibility of parole.

Cruz's trial judge had denied this instruction and made matters worse by instructing the jury that Cruz would be eligible for parole in 25 years. That "mistake" – if it truly was a mistake – mattered to Cruz's jurors, many of whom would have voted for life had they known a life sentence without the possibility of parole was an option.

Cruz's appeals seeking a new trial **repeatedly** fell on deaf appellate ears in the Arizona courts that incorrectly reasoned that **Simmons** had no application to Arizona's death penalty sentencing scheme. After years of more Arizona state court appellate sophistry, the U.S. Supreme Court in **Cruz v. Arizona**[10], in the majority opinion written by Associate Justice Sotomayor, intervened and reversed the Arizona Supreme Court and ordered a new sentencing hearing for Cruz in which he

---

10. No. 21 – 846, decided February 22, 2023. See also: Opinion: *The Justices halt an execution - and reveal themselves in the process'*, by Ruth Marcus, The Washington Post, February 24, 2023.

can inform jurors that life without parole is a possible sentence for his crime.

Cause for celebration? Vindication of appellate courts, the cavalry if you will, riding to the rescue of the Bill of Rights and *actual, authentic, real* Due Process and Fundamental Fairness?

Associate Justice Amy Coney Barrett, writing for the 4 dissenting Justices,[11] "reasoned" that fealty to the Arizona Supreme Court's sophistry was owed the "utmost deference", as opposed to any *actual, authentic, real* Due Process and Fundamental Fairness owed to Mr. Cruz or any other Accused. To say nothing of a human life that hangs in the balance.

In short, Mr. Cruz's life has been spared, for now, by the slimmest of margins: a 5-4 vote by nine clever wordsmiths.

These days, the U.S. Supreme Court, our highest appellate court – nothing more or less – and its Justices who labored so mightily in the service of their political masters to attain their seats on the "Highest Court", quake as their "prestige" wanes and public confidence in them shrivels under America's smoldering glare.[12]

---

11. Herself and Associate Justices Alito, Gorsuch and Thomas.

12. *Justices Grapple with Waning Public Confidence in High Court,* by Holly Barker, Bloomberglaw.com, September 13, 2022; *Confidence in U.S. Supreme Court Sinks to Historic Low,* by Jeffrey M. Jones, Gallup.com/poll, June 23, 2022.

What to do? What to do?

In the words of comic Lewis Black, "pretend to care." Canon 1 of the Judicial Code of Conduct states:

"A judge shall uphold and promote the *independence, integrity, and impartiality* of the judiciary, and shall avoid *impropriety* and the appearance of *impropriety*."[13]

Again, and as I've said elsewhere, "friends should speak honestly with one another, should they not?"

Friends, the Highest Courts, their appellate courts, and their various and sundry Disciplinary Counsel and Boards of Professional Conduct have turned Canon 1 on its head, glorifying the avoidance of the "appearance of impropriety" above real propriety, which is to say actually supporting the constitutions and administering justice.

So, in "pretending to care", the High Courts peddle the notion that the American criminal justice system needs "reforming", if only to salvage their prestige by putting the genie back in the bottle, lest a somnambulant citizenry stir from its repose induced by Madison Avenue's

---

13. Italics contained in the Canon itself. And, as we all know by now, the greatest irony of all is that this Canon and all the others have absolutely no application to the Justices of the U.S. Supreme Court. Hence the sordid political machinations of Clarence Thomas and his reactionary wife, to offer but one example of that irony...

intoxicating anesthesia of "culture wars", gladiatorial NFL and UFC "contests", and the promises of the "little blue pill". But to mix metaphors, that horse has already left the barn, hasn't it?

To the end of *somehow* clawing back judicial prestige and bolstering approval ratings, then, the Ohio Supreme Court, for example, from time to time convenes task forces: Joint Task Force to Review the Administration of Ohio's Death Penalty (2011);[14] Task Force on Bail Reform (2019); and Task Force on Conviction Integrity and Postconviction Review (2020).

The latter Task Force, spawned by public recognition that wrongful convictions and resulting imprisonment are shameful and anything but a rarity, actually held some promise of needed reform to Ohio's postconviction process. Alas, the 2022 election gave the Ohio Supreme Court a political makeover and once again drove the Court unto the tender embrace of its frequent dance partner, Ohio's "tough on crime" Legislature, thereby ensuring merely the pursuit of the ***appearance*** of reform.

And what was the net effect of these Task Forces and their thousands of person-hours and resulting reports?

---

14. Ohio's death penalty system was assessed in 2007 by the American Bar Association as falling short in a mere 93% of ABA standards for a fair and accurate death penalty system.

Absolutely *nothing* of substance.

Zero.

And this is entirely intentional, predictable, and preordained because Task Forces serve the end of "pretending to care", which is more important than actually caring, especially in the "Ancient Regime".

In 1960, after my family had been uprooted again, moving from Washington D.C. and the Pentagon to Sacramento, California, and McClellan AFB, the Colonel took me to my first game at Candlestick Park to watch the Giants play the Pirates. During warmups, Dad pointed to #24 in the Black and Orange and stated simply: "that's the greatest ballplayer you'll ever see." He was right; Willie Mays remains the greatest ballplayer these eyes ever beheld.

Willie's glove was known as "the place where triples went to die", especially after "The Catch" in the Polo Grounds during the '54 World Series.

Task Forces and large committees are the places where good ideas for needed change and reform to the criminal *injustice* system are, with malice aforethought, sent to die. To ensure a certain death, the larger the task force with its enumerable "stakeholders", the better.

Notwithstanding songwriter Chip Taylor's plaintive plea shared at this Chapter's outset, Chapin Carpenter's intonations are more instructive, aren't they? The cavalry, the appellate courts, aren't coming to save the day.

The sentient trial judge, endeavoring to fulfill her solemn promise to uphold the Constitution and administer real justice, knows that it's up to her to deliver ***actual, authentic***, ***real*** Due Process and Fundamental Fairness and that counting on *some* appellate court to make things right is, as Twain once remarked, a lot like "faith" – believing "what you know ain't so."

Because clever appellate wordsmiths are never likely to be lighthouses for the least of us.

3.
Actually Caring—
and Setting the Tone

"A lot more is said than is ever done…"

THE COLONEL

OHIO GOVERNOR TED STRICKLAND appointed me to the Bench on January 7, 2011, in the waning days of his administration.

Newly minted Ohio Judges are required by our Supreme Court to attend two lengthy "trainings" on a variety of topics, including Judicial Ethics, Evidence, etc. The training, from my personal experience, is excellent, owing primarily to the tireless efforts of Hancock County Common Pleas Judge Reginald Routson[1], the spearhead for Judicial Continuing Legal Education in Ohio.

At both installments of my New Judges training, I was required to attend sessions on Procedural Fairness during which a judge from the 2nd District Court of Appeals, my appellate district, first exposed me and my

---

1. Judge Routson is in the final term of his distinguished career. His shoes will not be easily filled, if at all.

fellow new judges to the ***Alaskan State Court Pledge of Fairness*** which reads:

> "The fundamental mission of the Alaska Court System is to provide a fair and impartial forum for the resolution of disputes according to the rule of law. Fairness includes the opportunity to be heard, the chance to have the court process explained, and the right to be treated with respect. The judges and staff of the Alaska Court System therefore make the following pledge to each litigant, defendant, victim, witness, juror, and person involved in a court proceeding:
>
> We will **LISTEN** to you
>
> We will respond to your **QUESTIONS** about court procedure
>
> We will treat you with **RESPECT."**

And who could quarrel with this statement?

The appellate judge, formerly a trial judge on the Montgomery County Common Pleas Court, encouraged all the newly minted Ohio Judges, his charges, if you will, to place this Pledge of Fairness on the door to their courtrooms.

Subsequently, I was again exposed to the Pledge of Fairness in seminars sponsored by the National Judicial

College (NJC) that I attended in Reno and Miami Beach.[2] Each time I was exposed to the Pledge, I resolved to place it on the door to my courtroom. And each time, I came home to Dayton, Ohio, and did precisely nothing. I'd make a great task force member, don't you think?

Until in 2017, imbued with a healthy dose of mindfulness following my Santa Fe NJC mindfulness training for judges,[3] I came home to Dayton and, after I personalized the Pledge to me and my staff, and my daughter Sarah – World Languages Department Chair at the Columbus School for Girls – translated the Pledge into Spanish, I instructed court maintenance to fabricate the Pledge and affix it to the door to my courtroom. The purpose of displaying the Pledge in English and Spanish should be clear enough: although a person observing the Pledge might read neither language fluently, if at all, the very fact it was displayed in something other than English would infer to the reader that the Court would likely get them a translator or interpreter to ensure fairness.

Notwithstanding that *every one* of my putative colleagues on the Montgomery County Common Pleas Court received the same Procedural Fairness training, to this day, I remain the only judge to display the Pledge at

---

2. On Drug Court training and Procedural Fairness, respectively.

3. My grown children had all "suggested" that I could use some mindfulness; hence my journey to Santa Fe.

the entrance to their courtroom. This is all the more note-worthy because the *very* appellate judge who exposed me to the Pledge *never* displayed it on *his* courtroom door.

Ironically, that very appellate judge, roaming the courthouse halls one day – perhaps from the sheer boredom of repeatedly writing that any error was "harmless" and that trial counsel hadn't been "ineffective" despite sleeping through the State's case[4] - came into my chambers, expressed his excitement upon seeing the Pledge on my courtroom door, and inquired as to "when the other judges would follow suit". I thanked the judge for introducing me to the Pledge and replied that I had no idea when my "colleagues" might follow suit. The judge appeared puzzled, and so I explained that I had acted alone, whereupon he inquired: "wouldn't it have been better if you'd all done it together?"

I told the Judge that I didn't expect to live that long…

During my so-called career before taking the bench, I was a trial lawyer. Nevertheless, courtrooms, for me, were places of great dread and foreboding. That dread and foreboding are magnified exponentially for non-trial lawyers: the Accused, parties, witnesses, and jurors alike.

Isn't alleviating and mitigating against this dread and foreboding the essence of the Pledge?

---

4. See Chapter Five.

George Floyd was murdered on May 25, 2020, visiting upon our nation, and especially our Brothers and Sisters of color, great suffering that was palpable and raw. Unless, of course, one was willfully blind to that suffering. At the time, former Federal and State Court Judge Jeremy Fogel[5] wrote in *The Recorder* that courts had an ethical obligation under Canon 2A of the Code of Conduct to speak out after George Floyd's death.

For some time, I had displayed in my courtroom various works such as John Lewis' quotation about having "a moral obligation to do something about" unfairness and injustice, Matthew Brady prints of Frederick Douglass, U.S. Grant, William Tecumseh Sherman, a 19th Amendment poster, etc.

I took Judge Fogel's admonition to heart and displayed in my courtroom artist Kadir Nelson's New Yorker Magazine cover of George Floyd, for which my then Presiding Judge promptly, and **without so much as a word to me**, referred me to Ohio Disciplinary Counsel, "dropping dime", as it were.[6]

---

5. Executive Director of the Berkeley Judicial Institute at the U.C. Berkeley Law School.

6. The complaint was dismissed and the George Floyd New Yorker cover still hangs in the courtroom. I speak to George every morning to begin the day's work and to remind myself of my moral and sworn obligations…

The purpose of displaying such works in *any* courtroom should have been obvious to even the dullest among us: to alleviate and mitigate against the dread and foreboding and to comfort, to the extent that I could, those coming into the court who were hurting and suffering after Mr. Floyd's murder.

During a subsequent criminal jury trial, an enterprising assistant prosecuting attorney asked prospective jurors to look about the courtroom at all of the objects displayed there. He then asked the prospective jurors to think of one word to describe the courtroom, and queried a woman of color in the first row of the jury box for her answer.

She replied: *"Welcoming."*

The prospective juror instinctively understood what my Presiding Judge had not: the artwork was intended to alleviate and mitigate against the dread and foreboding. And it *worked* as I intended, just as Judge Jeremy Fogel had written.

The Ohio Supreme Court was absolutely right to require that I and my fellow new Ohio Judges be inculcated in notions of Procedural Fairness. After all, isn't Procedural Fairness the very bedrock of our Bill of Rights embedded in our sacred founding document, the U.S. Constitution?

And by Procedural Fairness, don't we mean *actual, authentic, real* Fundamental Fairness, as opposed to something that *some* appellate court, *somewhere*, with a wink and a nod, opines will pass for Fundamental Fairness?

So naturally, then, trial judges throughout the Land, truly enabled and encouraged by their Supreme Courts to provide *actual, authentic, real* Due Process and Fundamental Fairness, do all that they can to alleviate and mitigate the dread and foreboding for all entering our courtrooms, by assuring them that they will be fairly heard, that the court's processes will be fairly and fully explained and that they will be treated with respect.

Not so much...

In October 2022, the NJC presented in Memphis a seminar – "The Anti-Racist Courtroom: Theory and Practice" – what the NJC proudly hawked as:

> a "*groundbreaking* four-day course combin[ing] embodied experience and jurisprudence to create a *deep emotional* and intellectual understanding of racial bias in the courts."[7]

Upon receiving the NJC's announcement, I promptly contacted its then Executive Director and offered to travel, *on my own nickel*, to Memphis to share my own efforts and experiences with *actually* creating

---

7. Emphasis mine. And it seems that the NJC too has fallen under Madison Avenue's spell ...

an Anti-Racist courtroom, including photographs of my courtroom. My offer was promptly declined...

This all calls to mind a favorite saying of the Colonel:

"When all's said and done, one hell of a lot more is said than is ever done."

4.

Friend or Foe?

Setting the Tone Revisited

"…The flag is flying high over the courthouse; the wheels of
justice never stood a chance; threw the ball to home, but they
always missed the tag; Faded Old Glory hanging like a rag;
If these guys are the good ones, I don't want to know the bad;
Defenders, Defenders of the Flag."

DEFENDERS OF THE FLAG - *song by Bruce Hornsby*

WHEN I TOOK THE BENCH IN JANUARY 2011, my *de facto* mentor on the Montgomery County Common Pleas Court was Judge Dennis Langer, former First Assistant to the Montgomery County Prosecutor. Dennis was a damn fine prosecutor. He was a better judge - smart, earnest, and, most importantly, compassionate and empathetic.

But what I admired most in Dennis was his unwavering commitment to an ***independent, co-equal*** Judiciary. Upon taking his judicial oath, Dennis "flipped the switch" and never, ever, slipped back into a prosecutorial mindset.

Every December, Judge Langer presented his seminar – "Criminal Law Update" – in which he discussed significant cases that year from the U.S. and Ohio Supreme

Courts, and noteworthy appellate decisions from the 6th Circuit and Ohio's various District Courts of Appeals. Dennis' seminar was always popular because it was good, and, more importantly, provided much-needed year-end CLE, lest one run afoul of the Supreme Court's mandatory CLE requirements. Upon his retirement, I undertook the task of continuing the tradition each December.

Last year at another seminar I'd organized – "What It Means to Be a Criminal Defense Lawyer" – the presenters, including Professor Godsey of the Ohio Innocence Project, Rachael Troutman, head of the Ohio Public Defender's Death Penalty Division, Judge Routson and I, much like this polemic, issued to the attendees a call to arms to *effectively* represent their clients facing criminal prosecution.

At the seminar's outset and at the suggestion of retired Montgomery County Common Pleas Court Judge John Kessler, I handed out 3 x 5 notecards to the seminar attendees and asked them to write one word on the card, either "Friend" or "Foe", regarding their impression of trial judges. I asked those responding "Foe" to provide the primary reason for their response.

I was unsurprised that roughly 85% of the respondents selected "Foe", and gave as their reason that "Trial Judges are in bed with the State", just as Judge Kessler had foretold.

But then you'd already guessed the results of the poll, hadn't you?

While the results of the rather limited survey are hardly empirically significant, they are revealing – and sad.

The reason for the impression of criminal defense lawyers that trial judges are all too cozy with the Executive Branch, which is to say the Prosecutor and the Police, is that *we plainly are.*

Sapiens are unlikely to change spots or stripes. It's in the DNA. If you don't think so, read Shakil Choudhury's illuminating book, *Deep Diversity* – Overcoming Us vs. Them.[1] Not a few trial judges are former prosecutors, unwilling to "flip the switch" because they are prosecutorial ideologues. I hold out little hope that my Polemic will register with judges of this stripe.

Others believe that the Police, Prosecutors, and Judges are "on the same team", sworn to preserve, protect, and defend, as it were, thereby explaining the allure of the *Reality Ratio*: better to convict ten innocents than allow one guilty Accused go free.

Brothers and Sisters, we *cannot be on the same team,* not if we believe even a little bit in our judicial oaths.

Some of us believe, *incorrectly*, that our task is to provide the State and the Accused with a "level playing

---

1. Between the Lines Press, 2015.

field". The Constitutions make it quite clear that the playing field is, by design, ***unlevel and tilted in favor of the Accused.*** The sacred rights enshrined in the 4th, 5th, 6th, 8th, 13th, and 14th Amendments run to the Accused, ***not the State.*** This is why the sentient trial judge ***must*** err on the side of the Accused, not the other way round.

However, I believe that the greatest factor contributing to the appearance that trial judges are in the sack with the State is that almost all of us are mortified by the specter of being labeled "soft on crime" by the Police, Prosecutors, Legislators, and an ever-compliant media, greedily rooting about for "clicks", like so many truffle dogs...

Ohio judges must run for office every six years, and many cannot resist the siren's song of blathering during every election cycle that they are "tough on crime" in judicial commercials and literature, believing that voters reflexively vote "Law & Order".

Each new election cycle illustrates the point. I am sickened by the advertisements of fellow judges touting their FOP endorsements as they appear in television ads with prominent ***uniformed*** local law enforcement officials. How is doing so not at least an "appearance of impropriety" in violation of the Judicial Canons?

I refuse to believe that the voters want their judges to be stooges for the Executive and Legislative Branches. Voters want to believe their judges are, in fact, fiercely independent of the influences of the other branches of government – the political hacks whose obvious and sole consideration is their re-election.

And guess what? I'm right!

In November, 2022, in little Dayton, Ohio, a young female Public Defender with no judicial experience, albeit possessed of superior academic and professional credentials, defeated an *incumbent* judge running cynically and unabashedly on the "Law & Order" ticket.

My fellow trial judges, resolve to fulfill your oaths such that when criminal defense lawyers are queried whether *you* are "Friend" or "Foe", the resounding answer is:

"False! That Judge is a steadfast defender of the Constitution, the Bill of Rights, and the American ideal in her administration of justice".

Just a humble suggestion.

5.

The Sixth Amendment's *"Promise"* of the Effective Assistance of Counsel—

and Other Mythology

"In all criminal prosecutions, the accused shall enjoy the right…to have the Assistance of Counsel for his defense."[1]

AT LEAST SINCE 1970, the United States Supreme Court has stated that "the right to counsel is the right to the *effective* assistance of counsel."[2] The Ohio Supreme Court and its appellate courts routinely echo this simple premise.[3]

If one embraces the plain language of the Sixth Amendment, were these pronouncements really necessary? For if counsel is *ineffective*, isn't that tantamount to no counsel at all?

Ah, but recall, Dear Reader, that SCOTUS is

---

1. The United States Constitution, Amendment 6.

2. *McMann v. Richardson*, 397 U.S. 759 (1970), emphasis mine.

3. *State v. Brooks*, 25 Ohio St. 3d 144 at 147 (1986).

populated by the best and the brightest from America's elite Law Schools, where the "knights of the keyboard" – to borrow a catchy moniker from Ted Williams[4] – develop and hone their judicial "philosophies" to a razor's edge.

As mere trial judges, most not matriculating at Yale & Co., we read appellate case after appellate case, allowing yet another conviction to stand, propped up by appellate fealty to the finality of judgements, because appellate courts have turned the Sixth Amendment's promise on its head, merely requiring that counsel not have been *"ineffective"*.

Indeed, in **Strickland v. Washington**,[5] the Supreme Court articulated the standard for ineffective assistance of counsel that is so amorphous as to be virtually illusory, setting a bar which my Basset Hound Wooten can clear quite nicely.

Two examples should adequately illustrate the point.

In **State v. Rosado**,[6] the 8th District Court of Appeals expressly claimed that, *somehow*, they were "not condoning" defense counsel's falling asleep during the State's case in chief. But the appellate court did precisely that by allowing the conviction to stand, despite defense counsel's nap manifestly inferring to the jury the defendant's guilt.

---

4. "The Kid".

5. 466 U.S. 668 (1984)

6. 2005 Ohio 6626

And in **State v. Williams**,[7] the 8th District stated that defense counsel's failure to call an alibi witness as promised in the opening statement was not ineffective assistance of counsel, notwithstanding that this failure essentially sealed their client's fate. How? Because virtually all trial lawyers concur that cases are won or lost in opening statement, with juries deciding in favor of who delivered on their opening statement promises.

In September 2021, I attended the NJC's excellent Program: "Fourth Amendment – Comprehensive Search & Seizure training for Trial Judges", taught primarily by Professor Thomas K. Clancy, a nationally recognized Fourth Amendment expert.[8]

At some point during the four-day Program, Judge Carlton D. Jones of Arkansas asked the attendees, all trial judges from around the country, whether they ever asked questions during Motion to Suppress Hearings. As judge after judge prattled on about never asking questions because "ours is an adversary system" and "I don't want to influence the outcome of a proceeding – I'm just there to call balls and strikes,"[9] I was grateful for my Mindfulness for Judges Training the

---

7. 2009 Ohio 2026

8. And author of *The Fourth Amendment:* Its History and Interpretation– an outstanding resource which no self-respecting trial judge should be without.

9. Or words to that effect.

NJC provided to me several years earlier in Santa Fe.

But notwithstanding my Mindfulness practice and unable to contain myself any longer, I more or less exploded and "suggested" to my fellow trial judges that, of course, I asked questions that needed to be asked to ensure that the outcome of the motion was just. For good measure, I stated aloud that which I have oft stated in open court and on the record – we are not *playing a game;* we are in search for the truth that will *affect the lives of fellow human beings.*

The point of this vignette?

Virtually every one of my fellow trial judges was perfectly willing to stomach *ineffective* assistance of counsel in suppression hearings. And this penchant to swallow constitutional misfeasance by defense counsel is hardly limited to motion hearings.

Frankly, criminal defense lawyers, retained or appointed, often go through bail and bond review, pretrial practice, motion hearings, jury selection, opening statement, direct and cross-examination of witnesses, jury instruction preparation and charge conferences, and final argument, all under the putative supervision and oversight of a trial judge, in what is little more than an elaborate charade. And to an almost certain result – yet another conviction that will be upheld in some appellate court as having passed, *somehow*, constitutional rigor.

For precisely this reason, it is incumbent upon conscientious trial judges, in what's left of an independent judiciary, to ensure the Accused receives a ***fair trial in reality***, notwithstanding trial counsel's shortcomings.

How, you ask?

In Ohio, Aggravated Robbery, a 1st-degree felony with an accompanying 3-year firearm specification, is punishable by as much as 14 years of imprisonment.[10]

Let's suppose the ***alleged[11]*** victim, robbed at gun point, is white and has had no prior contact with the Accused – a young black man. Isn't eyewitness ID, including weapon focus, so often a contributing culprit in wrongful convictions, front and center? And what about cross-racial identification, or more accurately, mis-identification? I commend to you the fine book ***Picking Cotton***: Our Memoir of Injustice and Redemption by Jennifer Thompson-Cannino[12] and Ronald Cotton about, among other things, the profound fallibility of human memory

---

10. I will not discuss Ohio's Reagan Tokes sentencing scheme concocted by Ohio's "Law and Order" Legislature which makes sentencing for 1st and 2nd degree felonies somewhat more complicated than this.

11. Remember, the Accused ***is presumed innocent*** and, until a conviction, using the term "victim" infers guilt, does it not?

12. St. Martin's Griffin, 2010. I had the honor of "meeting" Ms. Thompson-Cannino during a Zoom Seminar in which we participated during the Pandemic.

and cross-racial identification. Ms. Thompson-Cannino's cross-racial misidentification of Mr. Cotton led to his wrongful conviction and 10 years of imprisonment before he was definitively exonerated by DNA evidence.

Shouldn't a trial judge, truly interested in providing *actual, authentic, real* Due Process and a fair trial to the Accused facing those 14 years in prison, ensure that defense counsel is actively considering retaining Human Memory and/or Eyewitness Identification experts? And since Ohio Jury Instructions don't even touch upon human memory, cross-racial misidentification, and weapons focus, shouldn't that trial Judge, instead of relying on a jury instruction "cookbook",[13] be honing her own jury instructions on the fallibility of human memory, cross-racial misidentification, and weapon focus?

Shouldn't that trial judge insist that defense counsel's *voir dire* be tailored to the facts of that *particular case*, thereby inculcating the jury about what that *particular case* really involves?

What if, in the same case and *without* objection from defense counsel, the State indicates its intention to introduce at trial an entirely suggestive photospread from which the *alleged* victim "picked out" the Accused with 60% "certainty"? Should the trial judge schedule a pretrial

---

13. More on the profound importance of jury instructions in Chapter Eight.

hearing on the admissibility of the photospread despite defense counsel's failure to file a motion to suppress? Or shall we simply fall back on the "Ancient Regime's" stock-in-trade: "ours is an adversary system – we can't put our thumb on the scale – we just call balls and strikes"?

Together, we could go on and on with a litany of *"what ifs"* a trial judge might face in any particular case, including what that trial judge, actually honoring her oath, should do. But as I promised earlier, I'm not fly-specking here; I'm provoking.

In the end, if **actual, authentic, real** Due Process and Fundamental Fairness are provided, **it is the trial judge** who must provide them, by ensuring that defense counsel actually **effectively** assists the Accused who is **presumed innocent**, as opposed to expecting the appellate courts, ever subject to the caprice of political winds, to save the day and reverse a wrongful conviction owing to ineffective assistance of counsel.

6.
Pretrial Detention—
the Entrance Ramp to the Wrongful Conviction Expressway

IT IS ABUNDANTLY CLEAR that the denial of bail, resulting in pretrial detention, contributes to wrongful convictions and wrongful imprisonment, primarily by distorting the gathering and presentation of exculpatory evidence.

Why? Because pretrial detention makes it significantly harder for the Accused – constitutionally presumed innocent – to present a full and complete defense.[1]

We know this. We **have known** this.

But yet…

On January 4, 2022, the Ohio Supreme Court in **DuBose v. McGuffey, Sheriff**, in a fit of uncharacteristic clarity, held that money bail's sole **legitimate** purpose is to ensure an Accused's attendance in court and that public safety is **not** a consideration with respect to the financial conditions of bond[3].

---

1. *How the Pretrial Process Contributes to Wrongful Convictions*, 42 Am. Crim. L. Rev. 1123.

2. Slip Opinion No. 2022 Ohio 8.

3. Which is to say money bail.

DuBose was hardly newsworthy, especially since it was preceded over a year earlier by *Mohammed v. Eckelberry*[4] to the same effect.

Importantly, *Eckelberry* and *DuBose* merely followed the Ohio Constitution and the Ohio Revised Code, and yet they were remarkable in their rebuke of Ohio trial courts for clinging to the ancient practice of mindlessly imposing cash bail to ensure an Accused "marinates" in jail.

In pertinent part, Article I, Section 9 of the Ohio Constitution, as it should, mirrors the U.S. Constitution's Eighth Amendment, providing that:

> "...*Excessive bail shall not be required*...The general assembly shall fix by law standards to determine whether a person who is charged with a felony where the proof is evident or the presumption great poses a substantial risk of serious physical harm to any person or to the community."

Ohio Revised Code 2937.222, passed by the General Assembly and which must be read in conjunction with Article I, Section 9 of the Ohio Constitution, provides the mechanism for holding an Accused, *presumed innocent*, without bond in the most serious cases such as murder, kidnapping, rape, arson, 1st and 2nd-degree felonies,

---

4. Slip Opinion No. 2020 Ohio 4585.

and felony OVI, *if* the State can show by clear and convincing evidence that:

1. the Accused most likely committed the offense;
2. the Accused is a threat to a specific person or persons or the community; and
3. no set of release conditions can adequately protect those persons or the community.

Simply put, adequate and workable Ohio Constitutional and Revised Code provisions *already existed*, as noted in *Eckelberry* and *DuBose*, that provided a perfectly sane mechanism to hold an Accused without bail in order to protect the public *IF* the State could make its necessary showings at a bail hearing, the results of which could be immediately appealed.

And yet, *DuBose* unleashed a dystopian right-wing firestorm from the Executive Branch, flatly misrepresenting to Ohioans that a constitutional amendment was necessary to protect them and their families from marauding criminal elements and the liberal, Commie judges who'd released them without high cash bail.

Except, of course, *none of that was true*. Nevertheless, an ever-compliant Republican-dominated[5]

---

5. Owing to the on-going and unconstitutional gerrymandering of Ohio's Legislative Districts.

Ohio Legislature only too happily hatched State Issue 1, a ballot initiative to amend Ohio's Constitution to require – *require,* mind you – Ohio judges to consider public safety when setting money bail. And to wrest from the Supreme Court the responsibility to establish procedures for setting the amount and conditions of bail, placing that power in the hands of the Legislature.

What exactly, then, was the real need for State Issue 1?

The "need", Dear Reader, was to provide naked political cover to the three dissenting GOP Justices in *DuBose* who were on the ballot in November, 2022, and to enable another Legislative Branch power grab, thereby invading the clear province of the Judicial Branch.

Every Ohioan and American knows the Legislative Branch's primary, if not sole, mission: *getting re-elected, no matter the cost.* It certainly isn't actually making Ohioans safer.

Why would I say such a thing?

Because it's true.

Last amended by our ever-vigilant Law & Order Legislature on January 1, 2004, R.C. 2937.222 lists the crimes for which the Accused can be held *without bond* of any kind, including murder, felonies of the 1st and 2nd degree, and felony OVI.

Know what's *not listed* in R.C. 2937.222 as an offense for which the Accused can be held without bond in order to protect Ohioans? Try ***Domestic violence*** – the single greatest predictor of future lethality, thereby begging the rhetorical question: do Ohio's Executive and Legislative Branches actually care about protecting Ohioans who aren't running for election and in need of political cover?

Predictably, Ohio's "Law & Order" Legislature ultimately awakened to the reality that its hastily hatched and passed State Issue 1 threatened Ohio's entire pretrial release system – and those same legislative titans busily set to work cobbling together a legislative "fix" to override State Issue 1's unintended consequences.[6]

Lest I be accused of unfairness directed toward the Executive and Legislative Branches, our Ohio Common Pleas Judges Association were as church mice on the abomination that was State Issue 1. Perhaps our Association was fearful that standing up and asserting the Judiciary's constitutional independence and co-equal power could offend our Legislature – with its power of the purse strings – thereby imperiling trial judges' salaries and benefits.[7]

Or perhaps Ohio trial judges were fearful that they would be painted as soft on crime by the Executive

---

6. *Last year's cash bail amendment from lawmakers put Ohio's entire pretrial release system in jeopardy*, by Nick Evans, May 23, 2023, Ohio Capital Journal.

7. Meager though they be.

and Legislative Branches in forthcoming judicial elections, with no ability to fight back because the Judicial Canons of Conduct ostensibly prevent judges from campaigning for or against Executive and Legislative Branch candidates. That these Canons would never survive constitutional attack in the Federal Courts because they most certainly run afoul of the U.S. Constitution's First Amendment guarantee of political free speech is hardly the point. Try finding a judge willing to take on this fight.

Or maybe, just maybe, enough Ohio judges[8] prefer things to be done as they've always been done – which is to say warehousing and "tenderizing" the Accused pretrial, with no effective right of appeal, thereby "encouraging" pleas, even from the innocent, under the ruse of judicial economy...

Who can say?

This is for certain: no empirical study has ever shown or will ever show a nexus between cash bail and 1) the likelihood an Accused will show up for subsequent court appearances or 2) actually protecting the public.

Because *there is no nexus.*

Other than the obvious: an Accused, presumed innocent, but languishing in jail, unable to afford a high

---

8. Many former prosecuting attorneys.

cash bail, ***will certainly*** show up for future court appearances and ***won't harm the public.***

So, to hell with the Eighth Amendment's admonition that "Excessive bail shall not be required."

Which brings me to a philosophical comment. Ever notice how our sacred seminal document, The United States Constitution, is, in reality, little more than a cafeteria-style menu of "rights" from which our political masters just pick and choose those suiting their current political machinations?

Thanks again in no small part to Judge Routson, I came to believe fairly early in my judicial tenure that cash bail is essentially un-American.

To that end, and with the tireless assistance of my Chief of Staff Elizabeth Hall, I developed a ***Cashless*** Bail Pilot Program for the Accused who have no history of failing to appear and who are charged with low-level, non-violent felonies. In year 2 of the Pilot,[9] the participants re-offended and/or failed to appear while on pretrial release at roughly the same low rates as those of the court-wide pretrial release program.[10]

I would argue that the "failure" rates of my ***Cashless*** Bail Pilot and the court-wide pretrial release programs

---

9. November 17, 2021 – November 16, 2022.

10. Well under 10%, with virtually none re-offending violently.

aren't "failures" but rather "successes". And, in any event, recommend less, not more, use of cash bail.

And I'm pleased to report that the success of my Cashless Bail Pilot has reached all the way to Montgomery, Alabama, Houston, Texas, and Los Angeles, California, where I have participated in several discussions on the subject of cashless bail with judges willing to eschew the "Ancient Regime".

Recently, I gathered my Common Pleas Court's Pretrial Services Department in my courtroom to "inquire" about some things that were on my mind. I posited three propositions to them:

1. ***none*** of the pretrial officers responsible for recommending cash bail amounts to me and the other ten judges on the Montgomery County Common Pleas Court had a shred of expertise in doing so;
2. there is no known empirical nexus between cash bail and subsequent court appearances or protection of the public;
3. and their self-perceived role was "covering the collective backsides" of the Court's judges.

Every member of Pretrial Services answered the three questions in the affirmative. I was not surprised by anything but their honesty, for which I commended them.

And then I gave them all a hypothetical[11] case: recommending bond for a security guard at a Jewish Torah School who had, on a dark web social media site frequented by antisemitic vermin, issued terroristic threats against the very students and families he was hired to protect. I got recommendations for bail and bond conditions that were all over the ballpark, some not even in the stadium, such as Own Recognizance (OR)…

Again, I was not surprised.

Last Fall, Molly Gill, Vice President of Policy for Families Against Mandatory Minimums, penned an Opinion piece for the Washington Post[12] detailing some revealing statistics regarding recidivism by federal prison inmates released during the Covid Pandemic:

> "We are keeping many people in prison even though they are no danger to the public, a jaw-dropping new statistic shows…To protect the most vulnerable to Covid-19 during the pandemic, the Cares Act allowed the Justice Department to order the release of people in federal prisons and place them in home

---

11. Which bore a striking resemblance to an actual case in a sister Ohio county. Odd…

12. *Thousands were released from prison during Covid. The results are shocking*, by Molly Gill, The Washington Post, September 29, 2022, emphasis mine.

confinement. More than 11,000 people were eventually released. Of those, the Bureau of Prisons (BOP) reported that **only 17 of them committed new crimes.** That's not a typo. **Seventeen.** That's a 0.15 percent recidivism rate in a country where it's normal for 30 to 65% of people coming home from prison to re-offend... Of those 17 people, most new offenses were for possessing or selling drugs or other minor offenses. Of the 17 new crimes, **only one was violent** (an aggravated assault), and **none were sex offenses**. This extremely low recidivism rate shows there are many, many people in prison we can safely release to the community."

Don't these statistics strongly underscore that we're contributing to wrongful convictions through coerced pleas by confining many, **presumed innocent**, charged with non-violent offenses, who could safely be released into the community?

At day's end, setting conditions of pretrial release, including money bail for the Accused, **presumed innocent**, is vitally important, and sentient trial judges honoring their sacred promise to provide **actual, authentic, real** Due Process must treat pretrial release accordingly, even if the Executive and Legislative Branches, the appellate courts and the Accused's own counsel don't.

7.

Meaningfully Using Pretrial to Mitigate Against Wrongful Convictions and Imprisonment

WHEN I WAS 50, I was honored to attend the Justice Institute, the creation of Professor Joseph Tomain, former Dean of the University of Cincinnati Law School. Over the course of a weekend in Granville, Ohio, and along with fifteen or so fellow lawyers and judges, we read various literary passages and discussed their meaning as it related to justice.

And so it came to pass that I was finally exposed to Dr. King's April, 1963 "Letter from Birmingham Jail".

I lived in Montgomery in 1963, an 11-year-old boy attending John Floyd Junior High School while the Colonel matriculated at the War College at Maxwell AFB. Understandably, the Letter didn't appear in Montgomery's white newspapers. More interestingly, the Letter wasn't broached at any of the schools I attended thereafter, including the Iolani School in Honolulu, Oakwood High School in Dayton, Ohio, The University of Houston, The Ohio

University, and The University of Texas School of Law.

That I only learned of The Letter in 2001 at the Justice Institute was a resounding condemnation of the efficacy of my own education and underscored my personal lack of academic curiosity.

In 2017, I attended the Innocence Project's Annual Conference in San Diego. Much about the experience was eye-opening, primarily owing to the excellent content of the "cafeteria menu" of available programs on topics such as the Junk Science of "Full Room Arson Involvement," and the Frailties of Human Memory and Eyewitness Mis-Identification. Meeting Barry Scheck, Co-Founder of the Innocence Project, and numerous exonerees was an uplifting life experience.

In San Diego, I first encountered[1] the September 2016 President's Council of Advisors on Science and Technology (PCAST) Report, which recommended actions to strengthen forensic science and promote its more rigorous and thoughtful use in American Courtrooms. The Report's Summary put it succinctly enough:

> "Developments over the past two decades – ***including wrongful convictions in which forensic science has played a role*** and

---

1. Echoing again my lack of educational rigor and academic curiosity…

scientific studies of forensic science methods – have called increasing attention to *the question of the scientific validity and reliability of some* important *forms of forensic evidence and of testimony based upon them*... PCAST concluded that two important gaps warranted the group's attention: (1) the need for clarity about the scientific standards for the validity and reliability of forensic methods and (2) *the need to evaluate specific forensic methods to determine whether they have been scientifically established to be valid and reliable*...The study aimed to help close these gaps for a number of forensic 'feature-comparison' methods – *specifically, methods for comparing DNA samples, bitemarks, latent fingerprints, firearm marks, footwear and hair.*"[2]

PCAST was, of course, a product of the Obama Administration. So it was inevitable that President Trump's ill-fated Attorney General, Jeff Sessions, would essentially abandon the PCAST Report at the earliest possible moment, returning to the "Ancient Regime's" old ways of ensuring convictions – at *any cost.*

---

2. Emphasis mine.

This, in part, explains why so few trial judges are aware of PCAST, its Report, and its importance, and why so many trial judges continue to welcome Junk Science into their criminal courtrooms despite the admonitions of *Daubert³*.

But willful ignorance just might be another factor relegating the PCAST Report to the dustbin of history.

Trial judges must absolutely appreciate and embrace that *Forensic testimony* is often unreliable owing to "confirmation bias" as well as flawed, underlying methodology that has not been properly, scientifically validated.

Prosecutors, wrongly, often tell state-paid experts what testimony the State needs for a conviction, or at least a key element of the State's case against the Accused. As noted by Professor Godsey in his excellent book *Blind Injustice*⁴, knowing what's expected of them, the State's paid experts are biased toward reaching inaccurate results favoring the prosecution, in direct violation of the Accused's presumption of innocence and, frankly, fundamental fairness.

Hopefully, most trial judges look askance at bogus forensics such as bite marks, shoe patterns, and other "disciplines" not based on scientific principles with

---

3. *Daubert v. Merrell Dow Pharmaceuticals, Inc.*, 509 U.S. 579 (1993).

4. University of California Press, First Edition (2017) and another resource no serious trial judge should be without.

known error rates. But far too many trial judges embrace simplistic notions that, for example, finger prints are "the gold standard" of forensic evidence, giving no consideration to actually, rigorously testing the finger print expert's analysis and opinions. A sentient trial judge need only recall the FBI's false accusation, based on shoddy fingerprint analysis, that Oregon lawyer Brandon Mayfield was responsible for the March 11, 2004 train bombing in Madrid, Spain.

The plaque mounted on the front of Bascom Hall at UW-Madison proclaims:

> "Whatever may be the limitations which trammel inquiry elsewhere, we believe that the great State University of Wisconsin should ever encourage that continual and fearless sifting and winnowing by which alone the truth can be found."

This aspiration should drive every trial judge to fulfill their oath and to provide ***actual, authentic, real*** Due Process to every Accused, always, in every case, and at every turn.

Pretty good pretrial checklists for the sentient trial judge to ensure ***actual, authentic, real*** Due Process and Fundamental Fairness are the Innocence Project and National Registry of Exonerations statistics and ***the wrongful conviction factors*** detailed earlier in Chapter One.

The trial judge, then, must insist that defense counsel consider the retention of forensic experts to evaluate the State's case. But this insistence *cannot* be limited to forensic experts.

Recall[5] the daunting statistics of the first 375 United States' DNA exonerations? 43% involved junk forensic "science", 69% involved eyewitness mis-identification of which 42% involved cross-racial mis-identification, and 29% involved false confession. The conscientious trial judge must encourage and insist defense counsel identify and retain experts on human memory, eyewitness mis-identification, and false confession, as needed.

False confession, and the resistance[6] of trial judges to believe in this very real phenomenon, is revealing. The average person believes they would never confess to a crime they did not commit. And, if we've established nothing else, it's that trial judges are mostly average, if that.

Notwithstanding that most trial judges don't believe in false confession, the United States Supreme Court has, at least four times, given a nod of approval

---

5. Chapter One.

6. Again, see Saul Kassin's excellent new book: *Duped* – Why Innocent People Confess – and Why We Believe Their Confessions (2022).

to false confession expert Professor Steven Drizin[7] of Northwestern University's Pritzker School of Law and the reality of the phenomenon.

So, faced with an Accused's putative confession, shouldn't the trial judge inquire of defense counsel whether falsity of the confession is at issue?

The earnest trial judge should inquire early and often of the defense and State's counsel what *evidentiary issues* are coming down the tracks as the case progresses toward trial. Furthermore, the trial judge must require the lawyers to brief those evidentiary issues, thereby presenting the trial judge and his staff attorney with a *real opportunity* to consider those issues *long before the morning of trial*[8] instead of by the seat of the trial judge's pants, under the searing gaze of a seated jury, and the trial judge's self-imposed pressure to *appear* to command the Rules of Evidence.

Speaking of the Rules of Evidence, trial judges should conduct as many pretrial hearings as necessary to assure *actual, authentic, real* Due Process is demonstrated on the record. And how about *re-reading* the Rules as many times as necessary *before* the trial commences? I personally continue this simple practice that I followed for those 35 years as a trial lawyer.

---

7. Professor Drizin has testified as a false confession expert in my courtroom.

8. Or more likely in the middle of a particular witness' testimony…

Long before the morning of trial, the trial judge should meaningfully inform counsel as to the judge's preferences and practices during each phase of the trial.

This is particularly important regarding jury selection. By way of example, does the trial judge conduct jury selection entirely, or instead permit trial counsel to question prospective jurors? If the latter, how much time will the trial judge permit each side during *voir dire*? And if lawyers are permitted to question prospective jurors, the trial judge should insist that the lawyers inquire about ***the actual case that's about to be tried***, as opposed to merely wading in the shallow waters of the baby pool with nebulous discussions on the burden of proof and the presumption of innocence, etc.

My questions of prospective jurors during selection typically take 90 minutes, and I cover the waterfront of the presumption of innocence, the burden of proof, the credibility of witnesses, the frailties of human memory and eyewitness identification,[9] the prospective jurors' impressions of and experiences with the criminal justice system, sympathy, prejudice and unconscious prejudice

---

9. Unless experts on these subjects will be called, in which case I do not instruct the jury on these topics so as not to "bolster" the experts who will later testify. I once made this mistake but took to heart the 2nd District's proper "woodshedding" of me for doing so.

or implicit bias. Having covered this ground myself, I typically only afford each side 45 minutes for their respective questioning of prospective jurors[10] regarding what the case is really about.

The trial judge should inform counsel whether they will be permitted to use Exhibits during jury selection or Openings, etc. The trial judge should insist the lawyers who will be trying the case actually come to the courtroom and operate the audio/visual equipment several days *before* the trial begins. This is essential – unless, of course, the trial judge is amused by the predictable inability of counsel to properly operate the equipment.

Embrace Murphy's Law: if it can go wrong, it will. In the months, weeks, and days leading up to trial, trial judges must use that time to ensure the Accused's *presumption of innocence* is honored and that a righteous result obtains.

For example, make sure the Accused has "civilian" clothing, including shoes that fit *before* the morning of trial, and emphasize to defense counsel this is *their* responsibility. I once presided during jury selection in my stocking feet because counsel hadn't provided their

---

10. And yes, I would permit more time for the lawyers' questions, were it demonstrated such was necessary. My experience over 13 years on the Bench has shown such necessity is extremely rare.

client with shoes that fit. Since the Accused and I shared the same shoe size, he wore my shoes during jury selection. Except for a couple of jurors summoned to sidebar for a private chat with me and the lawyers outside the hearing of the other prospective jurors, no one was the wiser. Although I always wondered what those jurors at sidebar thought of the shoeless hayseed masquerading as a judge.

And, of course, all of the foregoing serves another important constitutional purpose: ensuring defense counsel is actually ***effective*** in the Accused's representation, even if the trial judge had to drag defense counsel kicking and screaming every step of the way...

8.
Jury Selection and Instruction—
Empowering the Jury and Enabling a Righteous Result

AT THE CONCLUSION OF EVERY JURY TRIAL, I take the time to speak with the jurors to thank them for their service. During this brief time together, I try to answer their questions. Inevitably, they seek assurance that their verdict was just, underscoring that jurors want to do "what's right", and look to their judge for that assurance and direction.

This is, of course, why jury instruction "cookbooks", like Ohio Jury Instructions[1] contain the following boilerplate for inclusion in a court's final instructions to the jury before beginning their deliberations:

> "If, during the course of the trial, the Court said or did anything that you consider an

---

1. Compiled by the Ohio Jury Conference and its committee of judges. I wonder aloud the percentage of judges on the committee who are former prosecutors...

indication of the Court's view of the facts, you are instructed to disregard it."

(OJI CR 425.35.02)

No sentient appellate panel believes that this little instruction actually immunizes jurors against all manner of judicial interference and intemperance, otherwise inclining them toward conviction. No, this instruction merely serves our ever-restive companion – appellate fealty to judgment finality – by giving appellate cover to the assumption that the jury followed this instruction, ignored the trial judge's histrionics, and did their duty, even if the trial judge did not.

Precisely because jurors look to their trial judge for direction in their solemn quest to do what's right, the trial judge absolutely must embrace *that meaningful, thoughtful jury instruction* is of *sublime importance* in affording *actual, authentic, real* Due Process and fundamental fairness to the Accused. And the sublime is not to be found in reflexively relying on jury instruction "cookbooks".

At the outset of jury selection, the trial judge must set the tone that the trial will be conducted with scrupulous fairness – and this requires never, ever, referring to an Accused as "the Defendant". If the young man accused of Armed Robbery in Chapter Seven's example was one "Robert Jones, Jr.", I would, upon entering the courtroom for the very first time,[2] greet him with the appellation "Mr. Jones". In any written jury instructions provided to the jury, I would initially refer to him as "Mr. Robert Jones, Jr." and thereafter "Mr. Jones", *without fail, without exception*. Denominating Mr. Jones as "Defendant" imparts a certain stigma, does it not? And there is no place for stigma in a courtroom.

And speaking of stigma, prejudice *and* unconscious prejudice, or implicit bias, have no place in any courtroom. The trial judge during jury selection *must* drive this point home by giving instructions like these:

> "*Mr. Jones*[3] and the state are entitled to jurors who will approach this case with open minds and agree to keep their minds open until a verdict is reached. Jurors must be as free as humanly possible from *bias*, *prejudice,* or *sympathy*.
>
> Let me address briefly the notion of *prejudice*.
>
> Prejudice is a word that has, perhaps rightly, taken on a very negative connotation in our society.
>
> But the root word of prejudice is "*prejudge*", and that's precisely what the jury selection process

---

2. And every morning thereafter.

3. Sticking with our hypothetical Accused.

is designed to do – identify prospective jurors who have prejudged *a particular case or set of facts and who, therefore, are* **not appropriate as jurors for that particular case.**"

At this point, I tell the prospective jurors the story of a law school chum who was injured driving to Townes Hall one day when a drunk young man ran a red light and broadsided my friend, landing him in the hospital, forcing him to drop out of school, and delaying his graduation. I explain to the prospective jurors that an OVI case likely wouldn't be the right kind of case for my friend, who might find it difficult to put his personal experience aside and decide the case fairly and objectively. I finish by explaining that my friend might be a perfectly good juror for another kind of case.

I then move on to discuss with the prospective jurors the notions of **unconscious prejudice and implicit bias:**

"Let me also discuss with you the notion of **unconscious prejudice**, *known in research and science as* **implicit bias**. *We all have these unconscious prejudices, operating in the realm of our unconscious mind – hidden or unintentional preferences for particular groups based upon social identities such as race, gender, class, ability, or sexual orientation.*

Whether we are aware of it or not, we are uncon-
sciously inclined to tilt favorably toward those
most like us and to tilt negatively away from
those we perceive as different from ourselves.
Importantly, our inclination to withdraw is
greater than our inclination to approach those
we perceive as different from ourselves. And our
brains are like Velcro for negative experiences and
like Teflon for positive experiences, which is why
political smear campaigns are so effective and the
news media dwells on negative stories as opposed
to positive ones. This negativity bias in our brains
is closely related to fear.

The home base for our emotions is that part of
our brain known as the Limbic Region which houses
*the **Amygdala**, the brain structure responsible for*
*the **Fight-Flight-Freeze mechanism**. Moment*
to moment, our Amygdala scans our environment
and spotlights what's relevant and important to us
in terms of opportunities and threats. This emo-
tional part of our brain works at lightning speed,
*processing **11 million pieces of information per***
***second**. Our neocortex, our thinking brain, can*
*only process roughly **40 pieces of information in***
***the same time**. And therein lies the challenge I ask*
you to confront during your jury service.

Because of our natural negative bias and tilting away from others we perceive as different, and because these implicit biases operate at an unconscious, lightning-quick level, our implicit biases threaten our ability to behave fairly and rationally in the presence of people we perceive as different from ourselves.

When implicit biases are unconsciously activated, two direct challenges to fairness emerge:

1. *we are unaware of the steady, continuous and speedy judgments we make about others different than ourselves, and*
2. *our judgments are not based on an individual's actions but rather the individual's social group.*

And because our emotional brain, the Amygdala, greatly outpaces our thinking brain, the Neocortex, we risk making judgments based on unconscious beliefs about social groups, as opposed to an individual's actual behavior."

At this point, I discuss with the prospective jurors what I refer to as the ***Philharmonic Orchestra illustration*** to explain implicit bias, noting that some years ago, philharmonic orchestras discovered an interesting phenomenon: nearly 100% of their members were male. How could that be, since physical strength and stature were hardly "instrumental" – pardon the pun – to making beautiful music? When the orchestras began "interviewing", which is to say auditioning, applicants behind a screen with no names, etc., virtually overnight, the makeup of the orchestras more or less became 50/50, men to women.

I use the philharmonic example because, of course, it is not politically charged in these troubled times of cultural warfare – and because I get a kick out of the knowing expressions of the female prospective jurors...

I finish my discussion of unconscious prejudice and implicit bias with this:

> "*IMPLICIT BIAS is real, and we could talk about it at great length as it relates to the administration of real justice. But we don't have the luxury of that time and we must try this case. I simply ask you to do all that you can to be on the lookout for your own implicit biases to ensure that they do not unfairly influence the important work you will do in this case.*
>
> *By a show of hands ONLY, and regarding, then, these subjects of bias, implicit bias, prejudice, and sympathy, are there any of our prospective jurors who feel that they*

cannot follow the law in this case and fulfill their duties as jurors, remaining as free as humanly possible from bias, implicit bias, prejudice and sympathy? (JUROR NAME) Bring them to sidebar."

My fellow trial judges, if you aren't inquiring during jury selection regarding prejudice, bias, and implicit bias, you aren't doing your job, whether or not these subjects are in your instruction "cookbook".

As a young trial lawyer, I found jury selection to be the trial lawyer's most daunting task. Somewhere along the line, I read Gerry Spence's excellent book, ***How to Argue and Win Every Time***.[4] The most important message of the book for me was understanding that my job was to fully empower the jury to reject my client's case, my client, and ultimately me. And that only by doing so would I engender the essential factor necessary to the jury's verdict in my client's favor: their absolute trust in me.

Finally, I threw aside the crutch of "yes or no" questions, learning instead to simply converse with my fellow human beings. I shared with them my genuine fears – for example, the fear of asking for too much money, concerned they would think me a caricature of the greedy, tasseled loafer-wearing plaintiff's lawyer, berated so long

---

4. St. Martin's Press, 1995.

ago by then Vice President Dan Quail, when he wasn't busily penning his Viet Nam War memoir: "30 Seconds over Muncie"…

By the end of jury selection, the jury and I were on the same team – Team Righteous – searching for the truth wherever it led us.

Because courtrooms are places of dread and foreboding for everyone, including jurors, as the trial judge, I assure prospective jurors that their service is essential and will, in the end, be one of their greatest life experiences of which they will be rightly proud. And I stress that, as their trial judge, my unwavering role is to ensure they have everything they need to render a just and righteous verdict, including expert witnesses, exhibits, instructions of law, etc., and that I will not fail them.

On March 18, 2021, in **State of Ohio v. Michael Sutton et al.,**[5] the 8th Appellate District for Cuyahoga County, Ohio (Cleveland) did itself and the judiciary proud and vacated, owing to numerous **Brady** violations[6], the Attempted Murder[7] convictions of Michael

---

5. Case Nos. CR-06-481840 D and C.

6. Imagine that! **Brady** violations! And from an Executive Branch assiduously doing all that it can to ensure righteous convictions…

7. Among numerous other charges such as felonious assault, firearm specifications, etc.

Sutton and Kenny Phillips, sentenced respectively to 46 ½ and 92 years of imprisonment. From my perspective as a trial judge, however, the most exhilarating aspect of the 8th District's Journal Entry and Opinion can be found first on page 54, Paragraph 143:

> "As counsel for appellants highlight, the **state emphasized at the original trial** that the defendants **could not prove a motive by police to be less than truthful** about the incident or **why defendant would run instead of surrender.** The Media is replete with news of police violence against blacks, especially young black males. **The statistical data is appalling.**"[8]

What, exactly, was the Cuyahoga Common Pleas Court trial judge doing when the State made these incendiary, illegal and unconstitutional remarks? Dozing? **Or, more likely, cheerleading for the Executive Branch,** pom poms and all…

At Page 55, Paragraph 148, the 8th District continued:

> "'[it] **takes a lot to overcome the practical presumption that police tell the truth in court,** especially when the competing story comes from the accused…The cases that come to light

---

8. Emphasis mine.

are those in which the evidence of corruption becomes overwhelming, which is most likely in scandals with many innocent victims…When that point is reached, the dam breaks and a flood of dozens or hundreds of convictions are recognized as unreliable or baseless."[9]

The unanimous 8TH District panel had the courage to say what every criminal defense lawyer and judge, trial or appellate, knows to their core: ***the State openly trades on the jurors' presumption that police tell the truth***. That so many trial judges give a wink and nod to this reality is wrong, and it's un-American.

Empowered by the 8th District Court of Appeals, I promptly fashioned a new jury instruction that I use during *voir dire,* again before Opening Statements, and lastly before Final Argument:

> "*Among the witnesses who will testify* ***MAY*** *be certain professionals such as ACCOUN-TANTS, CLERGY, DOCTORS, ENGINEERS, FORENSIC SCIENTISTS such as BALLIS-TICS, CHEMISTRY, DNA, and FINGER-PRINT EXPERTS, as well as OTHER PROFES-SIONALS including LAW ENFORCEMENT & POLICE, and TEACHERS.*

---

9. Emphasis mine.

*You, of course, are aware of the obvious: these professionals are human beings like the rest of us, and **ARE NOT** entitled to any **more believability** . . . **NOR ANY less believability** simply because they are a professional person. Rather, it is your duty to **CAREFULLY SCRUTINIZE** the testimony of **EVERY WITNESS** in this trial and determine whom to believe and whom not to believe. In order to do your sworn duty in this case as the fact finders, it is essential that you embrace the notion that no witness, **and the Court means NO witness**, is entitled to a presumption that they are telling the truth, nor are they entitled to any more or less credibility than other witnesses simply because of their calling, education or profession.*

*By a show of hands ONLY, are there any of our prospective jurors who will **NOT** follow this instruction of law and who will **NOT carefully** scrutinize and evaluate the testimony of **EVERY** witness, professional or otherwise, who testifies in this case?"*

I believe this simple instruction directing and empowering jurors to scrutinize the testimony of *every* witness, *including law enforcement*, is utterly essential to breathing life into the ***presumption of innocence*** and affording every defendant ***actual, authentic,*** and ***real*** due process.

I turn now to empowering jurors to understand the shortcomings of Human Memory, how it actually works, and its implications for scrutinizing Eyewitness Testimony, most especially Identification and Cross-Racial Identification testimony – factors that, as our Chapter One statistics tell us, contribute mightily to wrongful convictions and imprisonment.

Early in 2017, following an excellent presentation by Craig Stark, Ph.D.[10] at the 2016 Ohio Common Pleas Judges Winter Conference[11], I began the practice of instructing prospective jurors on the frailties of Human Memory. My first efforts were, despite good intentions, my worst efforts[12].

But over time, and working directly and repeatedly with Dr. Stark to refine my Human Memory instructions,

---

10. Dr. Stark is a Professor of Neurobiology and Behavior at U.C. Irvine's School of Biological Sciences and the co-Author of *The neuroscience of memory: implications for the courtroom*, Neuroscience and The Law, Volume 14, September 2013.

11. Again, thanks to Judge Routson of Hancock County for provoking thought among his fellows on the trial bench.

12. Much like religion, humankind's first attempts at philosophy were its worst attempts…

I arrived at the following which I unwaveringly give prospective jurors during the selection process:

"In your evaluation of the testimony of any witness, you should understand that imperfect memory is the norm.

Memory can be imperfect and is susceptible to distortion and loss because human memory does not work like a video camera – simply accurately recording events we see and hear that can be stored indefinitely and retrieved with perfect accuracy.

Unlike a video camera, memory can be distorted during any of memory's three stages: 1) memory acquisition (when a person witnesses or experiences an event); 2) memory storage (the period of time between acquisition and retrieval); or 3) memory retrieval (what is commonly known as "recalling" information).

*Exposure to statements, conversations, writings, documents, photographs, media reports, and opinions of others can all affect each stage of memory. Even a slight variation in the wording of a question can result in memory distortion. For example: asking "how fast was the black car going when it **slammed** into the white car?" can result in a memory of the black car traveling at greater* *speed as opposed to asking "how fast was the black car going when it **struck** the white car?"*

And although testimony may be given with a high degree of confidence and detail, research indicates that confidently recalled and detailed memories can be distorted, and that it is possible that less confident, less detailed memories can be accurate."

The Montgomery County Prosecutor "helped" me hone my Human Memory instructions – by repeatedly appealing my use of them to the 2nd District. These days, those appeals have stopped, perhaps because I'm the only judge using them. Who can say?

Inextricably intertwined with Human Memory is Eyewitness Identification and its common frailties, especially when one confronts cross-racial eyewitness identification[13].

I didn't initially appreciate the interconnectedness of Human Memory and Eyewitness Identification, but I'd already been instructing prospective jurors for years on the weaknesses of Eyewitness Identification before ever meeting Dr. Stark and working with him.

So it was with a sense of gratitude and vindication that I read the Ohio Supreme Court's December 29, 2022 decision in ***State v. Bunch***,[14] which stated in pertinent part:

---

13. Or, more likely, mis-identification.

14. 2022 Ohio 4723.

"…it has been well known for decades that any identification of a perpetrator after an initial attempt tends *to be unreliable*: The *very act of remembering changes memory*…"[15]

As noted earlier, Ohio is hardly in the vanguard of jurisprudential advancement. But perchance, did *State v. Bunch* portend that Ohio might finally be ready to embrace advances in judicial instruction on Eyewitness Identification, long followed in more progressive states such as New Jersey and Massachusetts?

What the hell was I thinking?

Following the Ohio Supreme Court's political "makeover" after the Bail/Bond struggles of 2022, its cynical 4-3 decision in *State of Ohio v. Johnson,*[16] extinguished any flickering hope for a more enlightened appellate approach.

In 2013, Eric Johnson was convicted of attempted murder, among other charges, based virtually entirely on his eyewitness identification by the victim James Keith. But in 2020, Mr. Keith provided his affidavit stating:

"…On a daily basis I have felt an incredible weight on my shoulders because I believe *I have identified the wrong person* as having committed the crimes against me."

---

15. Emphasis mine.

16. Slip Opinion No. 2024 – Ohio – 134.

Predictably, former Hamilton County Prosecutor Joe Deters, now an Ohio Supreme Court Justice, writing for the majority opined that Mr. Keith's revelations were too little, too late, and Mr. Keith's testimony, *somehow*, shed at best, a "dim light" on Mr. Johnson's guilt.

Is it ever too late to reverse a wrongful conviction?

And a "dim light" on Mr. Johnson's guilt?

The impact of Mr. Keith's testimony to this effect at a retrial of Mr. Johnson would virtually assure his acquittal based on the State's obvious failure to prove his guilt beyond a reasonable doubt.

Ah, but slavish appellate worship at the altar of judgment finality runs deep and it runs cold. Leaving Mr. Johnson with the bitter consolation that, were he tried today, he would be acquitted.

The import of all this discussion on Human Memory and Eyewitness Identification is, again, to empower juries to fulfill their sworn duty as fact finders to determine the facts necessary for a righteous result. To do so, jurors **MUST** embrace their role to ***meticulously SCRUTINIZE the testimony of each witness***, understanding that Human Memory doesn't work like a tape recorder, but is an adaptive process ***susceptible to alteration and distortion***. In days gone by, I instructed jurors to be "skeptical"[17] of the testimony of every witness. I thought that was the exact right word. My 2nd District Court of Appeals thought otherwise, rebuking me for using the term. Now, I advise jurors to "scrutinize" every shred of testimony. I know my place – more or less…

Neglecting to meaningfully instruct jurors on **every** salient subject, whether Human Memory, Eyewitness Identification and Cross-racial identification, false confession, etc., fails to empower the jurors to do their sworn duty and is ***the fault of the trial judge***, without question contributing to wrongful convictions and imprisonment.

Any discussion of jury instruction and selection must consider, even if only briefly, ***Batson*** challenges, again reviewed by the U.S. Supreme Court in ***Flowers v. Mississippi***[18] in 2019 and the Ohio Supreme Court in ***State v. Garrett***[19] in 2022.

By now, every trial judge should know that once a *prima facie* case of discrimination has been shown by the Accused, the State must provide race, gender, or ethnic neutral reasons for its peremptory strikes of potential jurors, after which the trial judge must determine whether

---

17. Defined by Oxford's English Dictionary as "not easily convinced".

18. 139 S.Ct. 2228.

19. Slip Opinion No. 2022 – Ohio – 4218.

the prosecutor's stated reasons were the actual reasons or instead merely a pretext for discrimination.

In determining whether, under all the circumstances, the Accused has proven purposeful race, gender, or ethnic discrimination, the trial judge must assess the plausibility of the prosecutor's stated reasons for striking the prospective juror in light of all the evidence with a bearing on it. In making these determinations, evaluation of the State's peremptory challenges must necessarily involve *the trial court's firsthand observations of each challenged juror*.

In short, my fellow trial judges, when it comes to the Prosecutor's "neutral" explanations for a peremptory challenge to which a *Batson* objection has been made, we know pretext and chicanery "when we see it", don't we?[20] And I suggest to you that the sentient trial judge, bent on providing *actual, authentic, real* Due Process to an Accused, cannot be shy about sustaining *Batson* challenges based on the State's fanciful, whimsical race, gender or ethnic "neutral" artifice. Doing otherwise guts *Batson* and contributes to wrongful convictions and imprisonment.

Carefully instructing jurors using plainly worded instructions that breathe life into an Accused's *presumption of innocence* and right to *actual, authentic, real* Due Process is absolutely the *most effective means* to

---

20. Much like Justice Potter Stewart in 1964 knew pornography when he saw it.

ensure "the playing field" remains constitutionally slanted in favor of the Accused, as the Framers **clearly intended** in the Bill of Rights. So I implore every trial judge to regularly revisit your instructions to ferret and root out the language of our "cookbook" instructions that, in reality, "cooks the books" in the State's favor.

Two examples should suffice.

I imagine every state has an instruction like Ohio's **Howard/Dynamite Charge**[21], given when juries report they are deadlocked in their deliberations. The following is Ohio's:

> "In a **large proportion of cases, absolute certainty cannot be** attained **or expected.** Although the verdict must reflect the verdict of each individual juror and not mere acquiescence in the conclusion of other jurors, each question submitted to you should be examined with proper regard **and deference to the opinions of others.** It is **desirable that the case be decided**...it is your duty to decide the case, if you can conscientiously do so. You should listen to one another's opinions **with a disposition to be persuaded.** Do not hesitate to

---

21. *Ohio v. Howard,* 42 Ohio St. 3d 18 (1989); See OJI CR 429.09(2).

reexamine your views and change your position if you are convinced it is erroneous. If there is disagreement, all jurors should reexamine their positions, given that a unanimous verdict has not been reached. *Jurors for acquittal should consider whether their doubt is reasonable, considering that it is not shared by others, equally honest, who have heard the same evidence, with the same desire to arrive at the truth and under the same oath*. Likewise, jurors for conviction should ask themselves whether they might not reasonably doubt the correctness of a judgment not concurred in by all other jurors."[22]

Is it just me, or is this "dynamite" charge entirely slanted in favor of the State and conviction?

Are hung juries really *"expected"* in *"a large portion of cases"*? Should jurors be admonished to examine each question with "*proper* regard and *deference* to the opinions of others"? Is it *"desirable"* that the case be decided, even if decided unfairly, by going along to get along and *deferring* to the opinions of others? Should jurors be told they should listen to the opinions of others "*with a disposition to be persuaded*"? Why? And why

---

22. Emphasis mine.

the primary emphasis on **jurors for acquittal** reconsidering whether their doubt is "reasonable" given that others, all too eager to convict, don't agree?

I recrafted the instruction and **might**[23]utilize this one in the rare event of a hung jury:

> *"In some cases, absolute certainty cannot be attained.*
>
> *The verdict must reflect the verdict of each individual juror and not mere acceptance, without protest, the conclusion of other jurors. It is essential that, if this case is decided, **it be fairly decided**... It is your duty to decide this case, **if you can conscientiously do so.** You should listen to one another's opinions with an open mind. Do not hesitate to reexamine your views and change your position if you are **firmly** convinced it is erroneous.*
>
> *If there is disagreement, those jurors for conviction should ask themselves whether their belief the State has proven Mr. Jones' guilt beyond a reasonable doubt of any charge is reasonable, given that other jurors, equally honest and who have heard the same evidence, and with the same*

---

23. I say "might". It's more likely I'll never give a dynamite charge again during my judicial career.

desire to arrive at the truth, and under the same oath, believe the State has not met its burden of proof. Similarly, jurors for acquittal should consider whether their doubt is reasonable, given that other jurors do not agree."

Which of these two "dynamite" options is more even-handed and not slanted in favor of the State or conviction? Which one will you give in the event you deem such a charge necessary?

For our second example, ***Consciousness of Guilt***, Ohio's "cookbook" instruction, provides:

> "**CONSCIOUSNESS OF GUILT:** Testimony has been admitted indicating that ***NAME*** (fled the [scene] [*describe* jurisdiction]) (escaped from custody) (resisted arrest) (falsified his/her identity) (changed appearance) (intimidated a witness) (attempted to conceal a crime) (*describe other conduct*). You are instructed that (*describe NAME'S conduct)* alone does not raise a presumption of guilt, but it may tend to indicate ***NAME'S*** (consciousness) (an awareness) of guilt. If you find that the facts do not support that ***NAME*** *(describe NAME'S conduct)*, or if you find that some other motive prompted ***NAME'S*** conduct, or if you are unable to decide what ***NAME'S*** motivation

was, then you should not consider this evidence for any purpose. However, if you find that the facts support that **NAME** engaged in such conduct and if you decide that **NAME** was motivated by (a consciousness) (an awareness) of guilt, you may, but are not required to, consider that evidence in deciding whether **NAME** is guilty of the crimes charged. You alone will determine what weight, if any, to give this evidence. (**OJI CR 409.13**)"

OJI indicates this instruction is "optional", but why give it at all? Presumably, the jury will hear in testimony that Mr. Jones "fled the scene", or "changed his appearance", or "remained at large", or any number of other things the State will advocate shows a "guilty conscience". Doesn't giving this instruction infer to the jury, looking for guidance from the trial judge, that they ought to just go ahead and find Mr. Jones "guilty". Why else would the judge have given the jurors this instruction?

And speaking of ganders and geese, if the Accused did not flee the scene, did not change his appearance, and instead cooperated fully with Law Enforcement throughout the process, would my fellow trial judges give an instruction requested by the defense regarding *consciousness of innocence*, inclining the jury to acquittal?

That, too, was a rhetorical question.

We began this Chapter at the end, discussing the boilerplate instruction that jurors disregard the trial judge's antics and any inference regarding guilt or innocence.

So let's end this Chapter at the beginning – the trial judge's responsibility during jury selection is to ***actually, carefully listen*** to the prospective jurors' answers to the questions of the court and counsel.

Not too long ago, a newly minted Ohio trial judge during jury selection asked whether any of the prospective jurors "knew the defendant"? A prospective juror indicated that she had seen the defendant "around town" where they both lived. After confirming the prospective juror didn't know the defendant personally, the trial judge, ***in the presence of the entire pool***[24] asked:

"You don't know anything and haven't heard anything about this case that's before the court, correct"?

The prospective juror responded: "I'm knowledgeable that it happened."

Defense counsel sought a sidebar, expressing concern that this remark might have poisoned the entire panel. The judge called a recess, presumably to review the record, confer with counsel and regroup as necessary.

Upon resuming jury selection, the judge proceeded to expound on the importance of giving the defendant

---

24. Rookie mistake 101.

a fair trial, and then essentially chastised the juror for merely doing what he'd requested: answering the judge's question in the presence of the other prospective jurors.

The judge then claimed that the prospective juror had stated "defendant did it", or words to that effect, and lectured the prospective juror on the gravity of what she'd done, including costing tax dollars owing to a mistrial.

Except that the prospective juror *had said no such thing*, as a simple review of the record would have revealed. She'd merely stated: "I'm knowledgeable that it happened."[25] And to her credit, the prospective juror respectfully pushed back: "I do not recall saying he did it, Sir. I don't think that was my statement. I said I know of the incident."

Had the trial judge taken the time to review the record, he likely needn't have ordered a mistrial. Rather, he could have informed the prospective jurors that any mistake was his and inquired, perhaps one by one on the record and out of the presence of the other jurors, whether they could decide the case based upon the facts they found and the Court's instructions of law, and render a fair verdict.

But that would have required actually listening to the record, swallowing one's pride, and acting accordingly. Indeed, the trial judge owed this juror an apology delivered in front of the other prospective jurors. Doing

---

25. My personal review of the record confirms this.

so would have demonstrated in the clearest possible terms to the prospective jurors that their trial judge was human and, most importantly, fair.

And the point of this vignette? Trial judges **must actually listen** to the jurors' answers to the questions of court and counsel in order to deliver **actual, authentic, real** Due Process and Fundamental Fairness.

Recently, I enjoyed a conversation with a gifted, seasoned Defense lawyer who shared that he now speaks directly with prospective jurors during *voir dire* about the very real phenomenon of wrongful convictions and the **daunting task thrust upon them to scrutinize the evidence** they will see and hear, especially witness testimony. This lawyer assiduously quotes the statistics I earlier shared with you in Chapter One regarding DNA exonerations, thereby illustrating to the prospective jurors that wrongful convictions are not the stuff of Judge Hand's and Associate Justice Scalia's "bad dreams",[26] but rather, an unrelenting reality. By doing this, of course, the lawyer challenges the prospective jurors to do all they can to ensure their verdict is righteous.

I ask my fellow trial judges: would you permit such a discussion with prospective jurors during *voir dire*?

And, if not, take a hard look at yourself in tomorrow morning's mirror and ask, "Why not?"

---

26. Epilogue.

9.

Evidentially Speaking, Are Most Trial Judges Incompetent, Indifferent, or Prosecutorially Inclined?

Evidently...

IN THE 1972 SUPER BOWL, the Dallas Cowboys properly thrashed the Miami Dolphins 24-3, largely on the performance of mercurial running back Duane Thomas.

Following the game, Thomas broke his near season-long brooding silence and deigned to be "interviewed" by CBS's Tom Brookshire in the winning locker room. When asked by the bumbling Brookshire if he was "really that fast", Thomas curtly replied, *"Evidently."*

Are trial judges evidentially challenged, routinely spawning a vast array of evidentiary rulings *favoring the State* and *inclining juries to conviction*? If so, are those evidentiary rulings the result of incompetence, indifference, or the product of a prosecutorial bent?

Evidently...

Recall, Dear Reader, the factors contributing to wrongful conviction and imprisonment as delineated by both the Innocence Project and the National Registry of Exonerations: eyewitness misidentification, junk forensic science, false confession, jailhouse snitches, and official misconduct.[1]

What's missing from the list of factors contributing mightily to wrongful convictions?

The evidentiary misdeeds of trial judges.

This is all the more significant because an innocent Accused is statistically much more likely to go to trial[2], leading to the inescapable conclusion that judicial evidentiary failings are disproportionately and adversely affecting innocent Accuseds with the temerity to assert their Sixth Amendment rights.

Criminal defense lawyers understand that trial judges, for the most part, exhibit a woeful grasp, much less command, of the Rules of Evidence, thereby inevitably contributing to wrongful convictions and imprisonment. The same can be said of most criminal defense lawyers. My friend and mentor, Judge Routson, believes that these evidentiary misdeeds amount to "death by a thousand cuts" – that standing alone, an evidentiary

---

1. See Chapter One.

2. *The Evidence Rules That Convict the Innocent*, Jeffrey Bellin, William & Mary Law School (2021).

blunder isn't likely to affect a trial's outcome or incline juries toward an Accused's guilt. But cumulatively, these evidentiary misdeeds are devastating.

Isn't the Law of Evidence all about **preventing** the admission of unreliable, unfair evidence that furthers wrongful convictions and imprisonment? Indeed, the Evidence Rules originated out of historical debates focused on the very real danger of convicting the innocent.

Judge Routson, an eternally thoughtful man, attributes much of the blame for evidentiary failings to an ever-increasing informality in American society, which has leached into the trial of criminal cases generally and into the evidentiary decision-making of trial judges specifically.

Contributing to the evidential incompetence and indifference of trial judges is certainly the United States Supreme Court's embrace of a **procedural** focus on evidence rules instead of a **substantive** focus that would pay closer attention to the lessons learned from the Innocence Movement, ensuring that evidence jurisprudence minimizes, **not facilitates**, the admission of unreliable, unfair evidence.[3]

Given SCOTUS' formalistic, **procedural** approach to evidence jurisprudence, the avalanche of appellate decisions carving out gaping loopholes in otherwise plainly

---

3. *Judicial Gatekeeping of Suspect Evidence:* Due Process and Evidentiary Rules in the Age of Innocence, Keith A. Findley, Georgia Law Review, Vol. 47;723.

worded Evidence Rules, *to the inevitable benefit of the State and detriment of the Accused*, is all but assured.

All the more reason why the trial bench cannot be excused, but rather should be condemned, for its lack of evidentiary rigor.

The substantive Ohio Rules of Evidence number only 62 and take up a mere 14 pages in the 2023 Ohio Criminal Law Handbook. *Let me repeat that: 14 pages…*

Calling to mind a simple suggestion – that trial judges should frequently read and re-read the Rules of Evidence, as I have done before every trial since my days as a trial lawyer, notwithstanding that I was privileged to study Evidence under the great John Sutton at The University of Texas School of Law.

If nothing else, frequent re-reading of the Rules would reinforce the Accused's *presumption of innocence*. For example:

> *"Evid. R. 103 Rulings on Evidence – Subsection C – Hearing of Jury.* In jury cases, proceedings shall be conducted, to the extent practicable, so as to *prevent inadmissible evidence* from *being suggested to the jury by any means…"*
>
> *"Evid. R. 104 Preliminary questions – Subsection C – Hearing of Jury.* Hearings on the *admissibility of confessions shall in all cases be conducted out of the hearing of the jury…"*

> *"Evid. R. 201 – Judicial notice of adjudicative facts – Subsection G – Instructing Jury* ... In a **criminal case,** the court shall instruct the jury that it **may, but is not required, to accept as conclusive** any fact judicially noticed."[4]

So where do those trial judges, embracing the Accused's **presumption of innocence** and thus necessarily erring in the Accused's favor, most frequently come up short on evidentiary rulings? Let's discuss several, although by no means an exhaustive list, of shortcomings.

Trial judges should stop the State's use of a hearsay loophole through which one could drive a fleet of Fed Ex 18-wheelers – the so-called *"Investigative Next Step"* Doctrine. Which is to say, permitting the State to essentially prove its case through repetition of out-of-court statements, otherwise known as hearsay, made to investigating officers to *somehow* "explain", or put into "context", the investigating officers' conduct during the course of the investigation.[5]

---

4. Emphasis mine.

5. This appellate sleight of hand goes something like this: the out of court statements aren't really hearsay. No, they are merely verbal "parts of acts" and are, as the acts themselves, admissible. *State v. Blevins* (10th District, 1987), 36 Ohio App. 3d 147. Talk about clever word gamesmanship...

Of course, it's possible that such out-of-court statements might be admissible pursuant to **Evid. R. 803** – Exceptions to the rule against hearsay – regardless of whether the declarant is available at trial or **Evid. R. 804** – Hearsay exceptions – declarant unavailable. But if not, and taken to the extreme, which is too frequently the case, the State hardly need call witnesses who *actually heard or saw the events* in question.

And that's flatly wrong.

The conscientious and independent trial judge informs State's counsel long before the morning of the trial that the Court will insist the State put on witnesses who *actually heard or saw the events* in question *before* the State's investigating officers unleash upon the jury a barrage of out of court hearsay to "place into context" the investigation. My uniform experience has been that, when insisting on the presentation of admissible evidence from witnesses who actually heard and saw the events in question, the State's "need" to pepper the jury with out-of-court statements to "explain" the investigating officers' conduct typically evaporates.

Said another way, why does the State have a "need" to "contextualize" the investigation, particularly if the Defense doesn't attack the investigation as somehow tainted? I can't think of a legitimate "need" – but maybe that's just me.

Trial judges all too often permit the State to introduce *"Other Acts"* evidence, which is frequently devastating to the Accused because the danger of unfair prejudice far outweighs the probative value of the evidence.

Evid. R. 404 B – Other Crimes, Wrongs or Acts provides:

> "Evidence of other crimes, wrongs, or acts is not admissible to prove the character of a person in order to show action in conformity therewith. It may, however, be admissible for other purposes, such as proof of motive, opportunity, intent, preparation, plan, knowledge, identity, or absence of mistake or accident…"

Not too long ago, the State's counsel in a Murder trial gave notice of the State's intent to introduce evidence of the Accused's Other Crimes, Wrongs, or Acts from an earlier case where he was found guilty of Felonious Assault in a drive-by shooting into another vehicle. To what end, I inquired? For the purpose of proving in the Murder case that the same Accused was guilty of a "copy-cat" or "blueprint" crime – firing into another vehicle in a drive-by shooting.

I denied the State's request and issued an order *in limine* preventing the same. My reasoning? Sadly, drive-by shootings in Dayton, Ohio, are hardly novel, much less a "copy-cat" or "blueprint" of anything.

More importantly, I knew that a "curative" or "limiting" instruction allowing consideration of the evidence as proof of "motive, opportunity, intent, preparation, plan, knowledge, identity, or absence of mistake or accident", but not as proof of the Accused's character and that he acted in conformity with it, was, like Arnhem[6], a bridge too far from *actual, authentic, real* Due Process.

Jurors most certainly take their oath and duties very seriously. They want to do the right thing. But they are human, and once hearing that the Accused had earlier committed a felonious assault involving a drive-by shooting into a passing car, his murder conviction was virtually guaranteed. The "rest of the story" is that the State had no difficulty in securing a conviction in the subsequent Murder case without the "other acts" evidence it had sought to introduce.

In order to test an Accused's credibility upon taking the stand, trial judges reflexively permit the introduction of an *Accused's prior criminal convictions under Evid. R. 609(A),* with virtually no regard for whether doing so runs afoul of *Evid. R. 403(A).*

A classic illustration of this mistake was committed by a fellow judge on my court by permitting, in an

---

6. A nice little village in Holland I've had the pleasure of visiting and the scene of the Battle of Arnhem in 1944 and the Allies' ill-fated Operation Market Garden.

Attempted Murder case, cross-examination of a testifying Accused regarding his earlier Felonious Assault conviction, ostensibly to test his credibility under *Evid. R. 609(A)*. The 2nd District reversed the conviction, ruling that a curative or limiting instruction to the jury that they could only consider the Accused's prior violent conviction to test his credibility, but not as proof that he acted in conformity with his prior conviction and thus was more likely to have committed the Attempted Murder, could not be expected to overcome the danger of unfair prejudice. To its credit, the 2nd District refused to engage in the fiction that a curative instruction could "un-ring" the violent propensity bell peeling in the jurors' ears.[7]

Indeed.

The solution was so simple, wasn't it? If the trial judge felt the Accused's prior conviction had anything to do with his credibility, permit the State to inquire during cross-examination of the Accused as to his earlier conviction *without naming the offense*.

Perhaps more to the point, what about excluding the earlier conviction evidence entirely because its minimal relevance as to credibility was surely outweighed by the danger of unfair prejudice under *Evid. R. 403(A)*?

---

7. *State v. Young*, 2002 Ohio 1815 (Montgomery County C.A. Case No. 18874). The 2nd District did good, those twenty years ago...

What of allowing Police witnesses to testify, somehow, as *"skilled observers"*, which is to say **Super Lay witnesses,** for which the State has no obligation to produce a report, much less inform the Accused's counsel of the State's intention to offer such testimony?

Evid. R. 602 states:

"A witness may not testify to a matter unless evidence is introduced sufficient to support a finding that **the witness has personal knowledge** of the matter…"[8]

E**vid. R. 701** states:

"If the witness is not testifying as an expert, the witness' testimony in the form of opinions or inferences is limited to those opinions or inferences which are **(1) rationally based on the perception of the witness** and **(2) helpful to a clear understanding of the witness' testimony or the determination of a fact in issue.**"[9]

I'm unaware of any "training" that police officers receive regarding the interpretation of tears, crying, trembling, etc., or that years "on the beat" *somehow* develop clairvoyance.

---

8. Emphasis mine.

9. Emphasis mine.

How can a sentient trial judge permit a police officer to testify, based upon the officer's *"training and experience"*, that an Accused seemed "unusually nervous", or "unusually calm", or any number of other things *entirely unmeasurable, untestable*, and frankly of *no probative value?*

When stopped by a Police Officer for some traffic indiscretion, are you nervous because the balance of power is most certainly not in your favor? I know I am.

Would an innocent person being interrogated for murder be nervous?

They should be.

Can the trial judge permit a detective to infer a husband is guilty of his wife's demise by opining that the husband seemed "preternaturally calm" upon learning of his wife's death?

How would such testimony meet either prong of *Evid. R. 701*, much less both?[10] Yet this evidentiary tripe regularly finds its way into the courtroom.

Before taking the Bench, I understood that police and law enforcement were experienced "professional"

---

10. The 2nd District (Montgomery County, Ohio) has stated it does **NOT**. See *State v. Hawn*, 138 Ohio App. 3d 449, 466 (2000). But compare the 1st District (Hamilton County, Ohio) case of *State v. Griffin*, 2003 Ohio 3196 and the Ohio Supreme Court in *State v. Hand*, 107 Ohio St. 3d 378, 398.

witnesses. Notwithstanding, I concede that a sincere officer might actually believe they *somehow* have powers of
"trained observation," permitting them to infer that, upon
learning of a wife's death, her husband's "odd" behavior *somehow* betrayed the husband's guilt. But whether
a police officer actually harbors such belief is hardly the
point, is it? It certainly doesn't make such testimony probative, much less admissible.

And, although less outrageous than the trial judge
filling the role of a second prosecutor in the courtroom,
how can a trial judge permit a detective to serve as yet
another prosecutor, making mini-closing arguments, etc.,
through the detective's testimony?

A very real consequence of trial judges' evidential
incompetence, indifference and/or prosecutorial bent, is
to enable the State not merely to invade the jury's province, but to usurp the jury's sacred fact-finding duty,
thereby contributing mightily to wrongful convictions
and imprisonment by allowing prosecutorial argument to
masquerade as admissible evidence.

The problem is at once obvious – ***Evid. R. 702,***
which spawned ***Daubert,*** mandates every trial court's
gatekeeping function to keep ***Junk Forensics*** out of
the courtroom. But no evidence rules are specifically
aimed at keeping out of the courtroom ***other junk
evidence***, including eyewitness mis-identification,

false confession, snitch testimony, and the opinions of self-appointed police "experts" that their witnesses are being truthful?

In the final analysis, for the trial judge providing **ACTUAL, AUTHENTIC, REAL** Due Process and honoring the Accused's ***presumption of innocence***, the most consequential evidentiary rule is ***Evid. R. 403(A)*** which provides in pertinent part:

> "***Exclusion Mandatory***.[11]Although relevant, evidence is not admissible if its probative value is substantially outweighed by the danger of unfair prejudice, of confusion of the issues, or of misleading the jury."

Simply put, ***Evid. R. 403(A)*** is the ***super gatekeeper*** that must be honored, at every turn, whether or not evidence appears to otherwise be admissible under some other evidentiary rule.

At New Judges Training in Columbus in 2011, the great trial judge John Haas of Stark County, Ohio, drilled into all of us the importance of conducting evidentiary hearings, on the record, and explicitly honoring ***Evid. R. 403 A.*** Doing so has never let me down, and the 2nd District, as they should not, virtually never second-guesses the trial judge who follows Judge Haas' admonition.

---

11. Emphasis mine.

Finally, trial judges should be immediately skeptical of any *"government created" evidence*, including confessions, out-of-court lineup identifications such as photospreads, and snitch testimony – and *Evid. R. 403(A)* should be *used pretrial* to screen all *government-created evidence* for reliability, long before the trial commences.

Any trial judge, being honest with herself, will admit that it's relatively easy to be a champion of *actual, authentic, real* Due Process and Fundamental Fairness in a low-level drug possession case. Confronted with a case involving a heinous crime, otherwise flawed evidence *somehow* becomes compelling to the trial judge, now confronted with excluding the flawed evidence or "letting it go to the jury", hoping that they *somehow* sort it out, even though the judge wouldn't.

There can be no more vulnerable or innocent victims than young children. As such, child sex cases are the litmus test, a trial by ordeal, if you will, for even the most sentient and earnest trial judges trying to honor their oaths and fulfill their profound constitutional duty to provide *Actual, Authentic, Real Due Process*.

How else to explain the McMartin Preschool sex abuse case[12] in Manhattan Beach, California spanning

---

12. Wikipedia.

1983 – 1990 and the resulting mass hysteria and moral panic *before all charges were dropped in 1990*?

In *State v. Boston*[13], delivered in the wake of McMartin, the Ohio Supreme Court reversed a defendant's conviction that he sexually abused his two-year-old daughter in a sweeping opinion reviewing the implications of the Confrontation Clause and numerous evidentiary rules. I commend the decision to you.

For my purposes here, however, I distill *State v. Boston* to its essence: that the trial and appellate courts denied Mr. Boston a fair trial by allowing experts to effectively testify that the two-year-old victim was truthful in her allegations against her father, thereby unconstitutionally invading the sole province of the jury – witness credibility.

Thankfully, *State v. Boston* remains the law in Ohio, cited again and again by the Ohio Supreme Court itself and its most respected appellate districts.[14]

Or does it?

In February, 2024, a child rape case commenced in the Mahoning County Common Pleas Court, revolving around allegations that, over seven years earlier, the

---

13. 46 Ohio St. 3d 108 (1989).

14. *State v. Davis*, 116 Ohio St. 3d 404 (2008); *State v. Wright*, 1st District, 2024 Ohio 851; *State v. Lillo*, 8th District, 2023 Ohio 2380; *State v. O.E.P.-T.*, 10th District, 2023 Ohio 2035.

Defendant forced a then four-year old girl to perform oral sex on him.[15]

Other than the testimony of the now eleven-year old child, the State only offered testimony from three witnesses who essentially **vouched for the child's credibility**: 1) a diagnostic forensic interviewer to the effect that there was no evidence the child had been coached; 2) a retired nurse who, upon watching the child's forensic interview, stated she'd developed a high degree of concern that the child was a victim of sexual abuse; and 3) the Case Detective.

The Detective testified, based upon his fourteen years of "experience" investigating crimes against children, that the Defendant's answers to questions asked lo' those seven years earlier "felt odd" to the Detective, because the Defendant was "prepared for every question." What, pray tell, Detective, was "odd" about that – since the Defendant had been notified he was being investigated for raping a four-year old girl?

Wait. It gets worse.

Under cross examination by Defense counsel, the Detective admitted **he had no training in the forensic interviewing of children**. Nevertheless, the trial judge

---

15. *Experts attest to child's testimony.* The Vindicator, February 9, 2024, and *Judge Sentences Youngstown man for rape of a 4-year-old.* The Vindicator, April 8, 2024.

permitted the Detective to opine that, in his "noteworthy"[16] experience, "…when dealing with a child under ten, it's super easy to tell if they're telling the truth or not."

How, in the arena of *Actual, Authentic, Real Due Process*, did this testimony from the Detective ever see the light of day, much less come within the hearing of the jurors?

Predictably, with the State's triumvirate bolstering the child's credibility, the Defendant was convicted and now stands sentenced to 20 years to life in prison. An appeal to Ohio's 7th District is certain. But what's the likelihood the 7th District will find that any error was harmless, and that the evidence of Defendant's guilt was "overwhelming".

My heart breaks.

---

16. That's a joke, Dear Reader.

10

The Constitutional Right to an *Effective* Trial Judge—

a Retrospective

MORE THAN THIRTY YEARS BEFORE Judge Susan Solle declared Dean Gillispie a "**wrongfully imprisoned individual**", and a federal jury in Dayton awarded him $45 Million in damages for his wrongful conviction and imprisonment,[1] Dean Gillispie and his lawyers were preparing to defend him in his June, 1991 retrial.

Gillispie's trial judge all those years ago was a man who'd been my senior partner until I left the firm in 1989. He came damn close to appointment to the Federal Bench by then-President Jimmy Carter. He'd faced withering machine gun fire at the Battle of the Bulge and was decorated by the French government for valor. He'd been President of the Ohio Bar Association. He was beyond reproach. I admired him greatly.

And yet…

---

1. In November, 2021 and November, 2022, respectively.

By the time of Dean Gillispie's retrial for allegedly orally raping three women at gunpoint, the trial judge *absolutely knew* that *not a shred of physical evidence* tied Gillispie to the crimes.

The trial judge *absolutely knew* that, in a case that was essentially an oath-taking contest, Gillispie *had passed polygraphs* denying he was the rapist.

The trial judge *absolutely knew* that jurors presume police tell the truth in court and would afford this presumption to the case detective advocating for Gillispie's conviction.

The trial judge *absolutely knew* that the three victims did not know their assailant and that their descriptions of him at the time of the rapes, nearly two years before the retrial, bore precious little resemblance to Gillispie.

The trial judge *absolutely knew* that, virtually two years after the rapes, the three victims had belatedly picked Gillispie from a *highly suggestive and tainted photospread* created by the case detective, after which he improperly told them that they'd "**picked the right guy**", virtually assuring the victims' false memories of Gillispie as their rapist. The trial judge *absolutely knew* that the State would use the suggestive, tainted photospread identifications to bolster the women's in-court identifications of Gillispie as their attacker.

The trial judge *absolutely knew* that Dean Gillispie maintained an alibi for two of the rapes – that he'd been camping in Kentucky at the time - but that the case detective denied, despite compelling contrary evidence, ever having the salient campground receipts central to Gillispie's alibi.

In short, the trial judge ***absolutely knew*** the ***stench of official government misconduct*** had descended and lovingly nestled onto the Gillispie case, portending a miscarriage of justice and yet another wrongful conviction.

And the trial judge, my former partner, a man beyond reproach, did nothing.

Nothing.

Read together, as our clever appellate wordsmiths never do, the Fourth, Fifth, Sixth, Eighth, and Fourteenth Amendments to the U.S. Constitution ***mandate*** that the ***trial judge be effective*** by ensuring an Accused, ***presumed innocent***, is actually tried fairly, free of junk evidence – such as unreliable eyewitness misidentification, and "**synthesized**" testimony born of official, government misconduct.

So, what should an ***effective*** trial judge, ***absolutely knowing*** what Gillispie's trial judge knew, have done?

An ***effective*** trial judge, pursuant to his inherent power, should have ordered that the grand jury testimony of the State's case detective be transcribed for the trial judge's *in-camera* review.

The Ohio Supreme Court has stated clearly that doing so does not violate the secrecy of grand jury proceedings, nor does it cause disclosure to the parties, the attorneys or the public.[2]

Had Gillispie's trial judge conducted *in camera* review of the case detective's grand jury testimony, the trial judge would have **absolutely known immediately** that the State had failed[3] to provide **Brady** material, both exculpatory to Gillispie and instrumental to his effective cross-examination of the case detective.

And speaking of the competing values enshrined in **Brady** versus those *supposedly* furthered by maintaining the secrecy of grand jury proceedings, here's a test, fellow trial judges: which values are more important in what remains of a once free society and to providing **actual, authentic, real** due process and fundamental fairness?[4] If you missed this one, consider polishing up your resume and scheduling interviews for posts in the Executive or Legislative branches...

Had Gillispie's trial judge reviewed *in camera* the case detective's grand jury testimony, what would have been the outcome at Gillispie's retrial? Does this question court mere speculation?

You tell me.

---

2. *Daher v. Cuyahoga Community College Dist.*, 155 Ohio St. 3d 271.

3. The State **absolutely knew** what its case detective had told the grand jury. And, in all events, the State is **absolutely presumed to know** what he said. Period.

4. *Wilson v. Sheldon*, 874 F. 3d 470 (6th Cir. 2017).

On November 21, 2022, righteous lightning struck the Walter H. Rice Federal Courthouse in Dayton, Ohio. Fully informed of the case detective's grand jury testimony[5] and the official government depravity that resulted in Gillispie's wrongful conviction and imprisonment thirty years earlier, a jury of eight, tried and true, returned a $45 Million verdict in Dean Gillispie's favor against the case detective and his police department.

This explains, of course, why the State fought tooth and nail to prevent disclosure of the case detective's grand jury testimony until the bitter end – the 2nd District's November 24, 2021 Opinion sustaining my March 25, 2021 Decision ordering production of the same.

President Kennedy once said:

> "The very word 'secrecy' is repugnant in a free and open society, and we are as a people inherently and historically opposed to secret societies, secret oaths, and to secret proceedings."

If only, all those years ago, Dean Gillispie's trial judge had been ***effective*** and had ensured that a man ***presumed innocent*** was provided with ***actual, authentic, real*** due process…

If only…

---

5. Which was at odds with the case detective's trial testimony…

Epilogue

"I can hardly wait until the Fall, that'll mean I only have six more Winters; that's the way it is behind these walls, you take it one day at a time; I can hardly wait until the Spring, that'll mean I only have five more Summers; that'll be a pretty song to sing, until the bluebells kiss the sun; and I can hardly wait to close my eyes and sleep with open windows…"

SLEEP WITH OPEN WINDOWS
Little Prayers Trilogy – song by Chip Taylor

"Because I'm tired of waiting for reason to arrive; It's too long we've been living these unexamined lives.."

MY THANKSGIVING – *song by Don Henley*

PERHAPS MY *ALMA MATER*, The University of Texas at Austin, got it wrong all those years ago when it rejected George W. Bush's law school application, no doubt placing way too much emphasis on W's mediocre undergraduate career at Yale and, perchance, a lackluster LSAT score, instead of properly "weighting" his "immeasurables". Maybe President Bush would have made yet another excellent trial judge upon graduation from UT which, as you probably don't know, turns out as many trial judges as any American law school.

Because, as you'll certainly recall, *then* President George W. Bush famously said of stone-cold killer and war criminal, Vladimir Putin:

> "I looked the man in the eye. I found him to be very straightforward and trustworthy…I was able to get a sense of his soul…"

Given this handy ability, a *Judge* George W. Bush, at the time of sentencing would have had no trouble "divining", as required by Ohio's Legislature, whether the offender had shown "genuine remorse" for his offense.[1]

President Bush is hardly alone in laying claim to an eschatological skill set. In February, 2023, The National Judicial College released the results of a poll question of its NJC alumni: "whether Judges believe they can tell if someone is lying in court."

A whopping *90%*[2] of the responding judges said

---

1. R.C. Section 2929.12(D)(5). Presumably other state legislatures, in their never-ending, crime-fighting flights of fancy, impose similar metaphysical duties upon their judges…

2. *Question of the Month* – Judges are confident that they can tell when some is lying, February 13, 2023 by Lizette Ramirez, The National Judicial College.

they were either "…very, fairly or somewhat confident" they could tell when someone is lying!

Or is this misplaced confidence another symptom of **Robe-itis,** that curious malady afflicting so many trial judges who, although rather unremarkable in their careers before assuming the Bench, after slipping into that "little black dress", became *somehow* jurisprudential titans?

In **The American Jury**[3], a survey of 555 judges presiding over 3,576 criminal jury trials nationwide produced two interesting findings: 1) trial judges and juries agreed on criminal verdicts 78% of the time; and 2) within the sample of cases where judges and juries disagreed, almost always the jury had voted to acquit **and the judge would have convicted.**

Do these results suggest that an otherwise unconstitutional, prosecutorial mindset has infected a significant portion of the judiciary, as we discussed earlier?[4]

If so, does a prosecutorial mindset explain virtually all of the failures of trial judges leading to wrongful convictions and imprisonment – from pretrial detention practices, to the admission of Junk Forensics and other evidence whose prejudice far outweighs its probative value, and to failing to meaningfully instruct juries on

---

3. Published in 1966.

4. Chapter Four – Friend or Foe?

bias, implicit bias, human memory, the frailties of eye-witness misidentification and the real phenomenon of false confession?

I think so.

In **Kansas v. Marsh**,[5] Mr. Personality,[6]Associate Justice Antonin Scalia presumed to "calculate" the total error rate among all criminal convictions at a mere .027 %, thereby bolstering his claim that the American Criminal Justice system "gets it right" a staggering 99.973% of the time. Associate Justice Scalia's "methodology" was completely and *intentionally* flawed, of course, because we cannot possibly know the total number of wrongful convictions to be divided by the total number of criminal convictions for any given time frame.

Associate Justice Scalia's inference that wrongful convictions and imprisonment are so infrequent as to be insignificant and beneath our consideration calls to mind the blather of Judge Learned Hand in 1923 that:

> "Our procedure has been always haunted by
> the ghost of the innocent man convicted. It is
> an unreal dream."

---

5. 548 U.S. 163 (2006).

6. At least according to my former law partner, Dave Rickert, who took an Administrative Law class from the "great man" at the University of Chicago Law School...

Perhaps we can forgive Judge Hand his sophistry from 100 years ago – he didn't, after all, have the benefit of the sickening statistics documenting wrongful convictions of the innocent.[7]

But what of Associate Justice Scalia and his acolytes, propping up Dickens' "Ancient Regime" and for "doing things as they've always been done around here". Surely a brooding, scowling judicial visage cannot be the lighthouse for our way as trial judges out of the dark to an enlightened and systematic rejection of ancient mistakes that condemned the likes of Rickey Jackson and Dean Gillispie to decades of wrongful imprisonment, or worse, for crimes they did not commit.

In Ohio, trial judges have at our disposal Criminal Rule 29(A) which provides in pertinent part:

> "Motion for judgment of acquittal. The court…on its own motion, after the evidence on either side is closed, **shall order the entry of a judgment of acquittal** of one or more offenses charged in the indictment…**if the evidence is insufficient** to sustain a conviction of such offense or offenses…"[8]

---

7. Chapter One.

8. Emphasis mine.

Said another way, when the State has failed to meet its burden to prove the Accused's guilt beyond a reasonable doubt, the trial court ***shall***, on its own motion, acquit the Accused. Yet judgments of acquittal are as scarce as hen's teeth.

I should know.

Not long ago, I presided over a jury trial in which the Accused was charged with Murder and Felonious Assault involving the shooting of two men at an illegal after-hours "club" – a "boot joint" as the vernacular goes.

The State, for its part, presented a fantastic story painting their witnesses as ***unarmed*** paragons of virtue – notwithstanding that all three were Club "security" personnel – who testified that the Accused provoked a fight with one of the Club's bouncers. Per the State's witnesses, the Accused, taking a beating, pulled a handgun from his waist band and proceeded to fire multiple shots in the direction of the deceased victim who was merely playing the role of peacemaker[9] by pulling the bouncer off of the Accused.

Except that the State's Evidence Crew found only two spent shell casings in the side yard where the killing took place: one casing from the Accused's gun and one casing from the area where the victim had dragged the "unarmed" bouncer to break up the fight. Hmmm…

---

9. That much of the State's case rang true: the deceased victim was trying to break up the fight.

Not unimportantly, the Evidence Crew found 6 shell casings from the Accused's 9 mm handgun – the one in the side yard where the deceased peacemaker was killed, and 5 more some considerable distance away and in the street as the Accused, under a hail of gun fire, fled.

The Evidence Crew and ballistics confirmed that 3 "mystery" guns – none ever recovered – had fired 15 shots toward the Accused as he fled. One of the "mystery" guns, a .45 caliber, had fired a single shot from the back of the side yard where the peacemaker had dragged the "unarmed" bouncer, and 4 more shots near the street at the Accused as he fled. Surely, it's not lost on the Reader that 1) the 3 "Club" employees all denied being armed and yet 2) the Evidence Crew and subsequent ballistics confirmed 3 "mystery" guns had fired shots at the scene...

The Accused took the stand and testified he had fired in self-defense, first the single shot[10] in the side yard, and then 5 more as he fled, under withering fire, across the street to safety. The Accused also admitted he'd lied to the police during interrogation when he denied having a gun, much less firing one.

After charging the jury, I struggled with something I've never done: ***on my own motion*** granting a Rule 29

---

10. Which killed the victim.

Motion for Acquittal.[11] I should have done it – because if there was ever a case where the State had failed to meet its burden of proof, this was it. In fact, I correctly predicted a Defense verdict, owing to the glaring flaws in the State's case, particularly as to who'd fired the first shot.

The jury acquitted because, as they told me later, they couldn't decide "who'd fired first" and the State had necessarily failed to meet its burden to prove the Defendant hadn't fired in self-defense. The jury had done their duty, even if I hadn't done mine.

I flinched. Failed, really. Why?

Socrates, "his ownself", said "an unexamined life isn't worth living." I quoted Don Henley to this effect at the outset of this "goodbye", given that he hails from Gilmer, Texas, shares my birthday, and I spend more time with him than Socrates…

I'd like to think that, had the jury convicted the Accused, I would have granted a judgment of acquittal. But trying to live an "examined" life, I wonder. Would I have summoned the courage, in the face of a guilty verdict, and ordered acquittal? Or would I have taken "safe harbor" behind sweet appellate nothings that I must construe the evidence most favorably to the State,[12] especially

---

11. Presumably other States have provisions for Acquittal Motions as enshrined in Ohio Cr. R. 29.

12. *State v. Hopfer*, 112 Ohio App. 3d 521 (2nd District; 1996).

since the Accused, after all, had lied to the Police and must, then, be lying about who fired first. And while we're at it, how does the appellate admonition to construe the evidence most favorably to the State comport with the Accused's presumption of evidence?

As a trial judge, there can be no greater burden to take to the grave than the knowledge that one has contributed to a wrongful conviction of an innocent Accused.

I stand by my indictment of trial judges as the greatest cause of wrongful convictions and imprisonment.

We don't ensure ***effective*** representation of the Accused. We don't fulfill the 8th Amendment's mandate not to impose ***excessive bail.*** We don't employ pretrial practices to fulfill our ***gatekeeping*** responsibilities including the retention of necessary experts and screening of ***government created*** evidence. We most certainly don't ***meaningfully instruct jurors***, thereby failing to empower and enable them to fulfill their sacred duties, and we don't gird ourselves for inevitable ***evidentiary rulings.***

Collectively, these failures by the trial judge ensure that ***actual, authentic, real*** Due Process and Fundamental Fairness are not delivered to the Accused, and these failures most certainly contribute to, if not downright cause, wrongful convictions.

But I also insist that trial judges are the ***only real solution*** to the evils of wrongful convictions and imprisonment. Those solutions certainly aren't coming from the Appellate Courts, much less the Executive or Legislative Branches.

Recently the NJC released the results of its poll whether judges have confidence in the US Supreme Court. Only 1 in 3 responding judges said they had "a great deal" or "quite a lot" of confidence in the High Court. *4 in 10 responding judges indicated they had "very little" confidence in the Court.*[13]

And so there is reason for optimism that trial judges know Dickens' "Ancient Regime" must change and that the High Courts are not the engine for that change. Rather, *it's the trial judges* who must do the heavy lifting of ensuring *actual, authentic, real* Due Process and Fundamental Fairness are provided to the Accused at every turn.

Singer-songwriter Don Williams[14] sang a little song that resonates with me. Maybe it will with you, too:

> "...*And I've got a broken heart; But I've come this far, and I ain't givin' up;*
>
> *I pray for a bigger heart; I pray for the will to keep on walking when the way is dark; I follow that winding road, just trying to stay on track. I don't*

---

13. *Question of the Month* – National Judicial College – June 30, 2023.

14. Stronger Back — song by Don Williams.

pray for a lighter load, I pray for a stronger back."

So, to all of us toiling in the law's vineyards, may we renew each day our oaths of office and breathe life into the Constitutions such that **Blackstone's Ratio** becomes the American Reality, and, in the process, we reclaim our very souls.

Suggested Reading

Blind Injustice: A Former Prosecutor Exposes the Psychology and Politics of Wrongful Convictions, by Mark Godsey, University of California Press, First Edition (2017)

Deep Diversity: Overcoming Us vs. Them, by Shakil Choudhury, Between the Lines Press (2015)

Duped: Why Innocent People Confess – and Why We Believe Their Confessions, by Saul Kassin Phd. D., Prometheus (2022)

How to Argue and Win Every Time, by Gerry Spence, St. Martins (1995)

Picking Cotton: Our Memoir of Injustice and Redemption, by Jennifer Thompson-Cannino, Ronald Cotton and Erin Torneo, St. Martin's Griffin (2010)

Presumed Guilty: How the Supreme Court Empowered the Police and Subverted Civil Rights, by Erwin Chemerinsky, Liveright Publishing (2021)

The Faces of Poverty in North Carolina, by Gene R. Nichol, University of North Carolina Press (2021)

The Fourth Amendment: Its History and Interpretation, by Thomas K. Clancy, Carolina Academic Press, Third Edition (2017)

The Neuroscience of Memory: implications for the courtroom, by Joyce W. Lacy and Craig E.L. Stark, Neuroscience and the Law – Science and Society, Vol. 14, September, 2013

Usual Cruelty: The Complicity of Lawyers in the Criminal Injustice System, by Alec Karakatsanis, The New Press (2019)

Why the Dreyfus Affair Matters, by Louis Begley, Yale University Press (2009)

Acknowledgements

THE BEST PART of *Extreme Cruelty* might be its cover, designed by my wife Nancy.

To the extent that this little book presents any grammatical or typographical errors, no blame lies with my legion of tireless proofreaders, including my wife Nancy, my Chief of Staff Elizabeth Hall, son-in-law John Harvey, and numerous others. The fault is entirely my own.

Lawyer Alicia Diaz provided helpful research when necessary.

While the "**idea**" for the book was mine, UC Law Professor and Ohio Innocence Project Director Mark Godsey and Hancock County Ohio Common Pleas Judge Reginald Routson were instrumental in their unwavering support of the project, and especially their invaluable hints that helped make this book as good as my capabilities permitted.

Others like retired Montgomery County Ohio Common Pleas Judges John "Jack" Meagher and John Kessler, Akron Law Professor Dana Cole, law school friend and fellow plaintiffs' lawyer Joe Crews of Austin, and lawyers Jay Adams and Larry Greger provided insightful suggestions.

Authors and friends Wil Haygood ("*Showdown*" and "*Colorization*"), Gilbert King ("*Devil in the Grove*" and "*Beneath a Ruthless Sun*"), and UNC-Chapel Hill Law Professor Gene Nichol ("*The Faces of Poverty in North Carolina*") continually inspire an old man journeying toward ***actual, authentic, real*** fundamental fairness.

For Barry, Bill, Bob, Brent, Bryce, Eric, Jeff, John G, John P, Jim, Lew, Scott, and Willie. You don't need many friends – just good ones.

And for the Colonel, Carl, George, Grafton, John W., Russ, and especially Krummie – I miss you all.

About the Author

JUDGE STEVEN K. DANKOF, SR. is a General Division judge on the Montgomery County, Ohio Common Pleas Court, serving continuously since January, 2011, following his appointment to the Bench by then Ohio Governor Ted Strickland.

Judge Dankof graduated *Summa Cum Laude* from The Ohio University in 1973 and graduated with Honors from The University of Texas at Austin's School of Law (Townes Hall) in 1976 where he received The Order of the Coif.

Upon graduation from law school, Judge Dankof was a practicing plaintiffs' and criminal defense trial lawyer in Dayton, Ohio for 35 years before his appointment to the Bench. Judge Dankof has lectured for numerous organizations including the Ohio Common Pleas Judges Association, the Dayton and Ohio State Bar Associations, and the University of Cincinnati Honors College and School of Law.

Printed in Great Britain
by Amazon

47454137R00086